NEW MEXICO
CUISINE

NEW MEXICO CUISINE

Recipes from the Land of Enchantment

CLYDE CASEY

Clear Light Publishing
Santa Fe, New Mexico

First Edition
10 9 8 7 6 5 4 3 2 1

Library of Congress Cataloging-in-Publication Data

Casey, Clyde.
  New Mexico cuisine : recipes from the Land of Enchantment / Clyde Casey. — 1st ed.
      p. cm.
  Includes index.
  ISBN-13: 978-1-57416-096-3
  ISBN-10: 1-57416-096-6
  1. Cookery, American—Southwestern style. 2. Cookery—New Mexico. 3. New Mexico—Social life and customs. 4. New Mexico—Description and travel. I. Title.

  TX715.2.S69C3823 2009
  641.59789—dc22

                                                        2009010897
Front cover design: Gregory Lucero
Interior design & typography: Gregory Lucero

TABLE OF CONTENTS

Introduction

Breads   55

Main Dishes   71

Vegetables and Side Dishes 107

Chili 121

Dedication:

To My Wife Millie

For over 50 years my loving companion,

Without whom my life would have little meaning

INTRODUCTION

It all started many years ago, when I was a guest for lunch at the Pink Adobe Restaurant in Santa Fe, New Mexico. Surrounded by thick adobe walls and Southwestern ambience, I was served a trio of dishes made from chile, beans and corn, dressed with green chile sauce and cheese—and I was hooked. It was an instant love affair that has lasted over forty years. The clear assertive flavors and bright colors coupled with a sassy heat gave me an appetite and true appreciation for this festive food, known throughout the world as "New Mexico Cuisine."

My first cookbook of New Mexico recipes, *New Mexico Cooking: Southwest Flavors of the Past and Present*, was published in 1994 and has been out of print for several years. Since then I have written two other cookbooks, including the best-selling *Red or Green: New Mexico Cuisine*. This new cookbook, my fourth, features dozens of new recipes designed for today's `quick and convenient lifestyle, as well as a few traditional ones carefully selected from my first—now out-of-print—cookbook. I have included some quick recipes as well as some that require time and patience. Each has its place, because you will find, as I have, that the more you prepare this cuisine, the more you will want to be challenged.

Traditional New Mexico food is based Pueblo Indian cuisine, historically a combination of chile, corn, beans, squash, wild fruits, nuts and game meat. Many consider it to be America's oldest culinary heritage, with roots that can be traced back to the Ancestral Puebloans who inhabited the Four Corners area around a thousand years ago. As what was to become New Mexico slowly became populated with people from other cultures, the food underwent corresponding changes. This began with the arrival of the Spaniards in the early 1500s. They found the indigenous Pueblo Indians cleverly using nearly all of the edible plants and animals available. The Spaniards brought chickens, pigs, cattle, olives, grapes, rice, sugar, wheat, ground cinnamon and a variety of other spices. Later, in the mid-1800s, the French influence blended with the Spanish and Indian to create a rich, delicate, very diverse yet distinctive style. Today, the rich fusion of many culinary traditions — and the innovations of some modern chefs — have given us a cuisine that is a blend of Pueblo Indian, Spanish, Mexican, Tex-Mex, Cowboy Chuckwagon, French and Mediterranean influences. The surprising result of the melding of these traditional ethnic and imported specialties in unusual varieties and combinations is a cuisine found nowhere else in the world. New Mexico cuisine is distinctly different from that of other Southwestern areas, even from the neighboring states of Texas and Arizona.

CHILE PEPPERS
The Fire in New Mexico Cooking

The chile pepper, the *fire* in New Mexico cooking, is a vegetable, not a spice. I will never forget the delightful smell of roasting chiles I encountered during my first trip to one of several chile pepper farms just outside Roswell, New Mexico. Here folks create strings of the brilliant red chiles, called *ristras,* and hang them to dry outside their homes as signs of welcome or decoration. Hanging in the kitchens of some homes are strings of chiles used for everyday cooking. They just pluck one off and grind it up as a food additive for every thing from pizza to a topping for hors d'oeuvres. Images of these colorful peppers are found on everything from Christmas decorations to men's underwear.

Health Benefits of Chile Peppers

In addition to decorating homes and enhancing the flavor of foods, chile peppers apparently have many relatively unknown health benefits. Capsaicin (8-methyl-N-vanillyl-6-nonenamide) is the chemical substance found in all chile peppers. This oily orange-colored acid, found in the seeds and veins, gives the chile pepper its piquancy, which can range from innocent to outright incendiary. When ingested, the stimulation of the capsaicin produces a release of endorphins, the body's natural painkillers, resulting in a sensation of pleasure. This feeling of well-being can become addictive and explains the reason why chile lovers must have their fix, and the more chile they eat, the more they crave. Topical application also appears to be helpful in pain relief, because capsaicin inhibits substance P, an amino acid peptide associated with pain.

Every year new healthful properties of chiles continue to be discovered. It is now known that capsaicin can prevent cancer development in animal models and cause cancer cell death in cultured tumor cells from oxygen starvation due to its presence. Recent experiments indicate capsaicin may also be very useful in the treatment of diabetic neuropathy (nerve pain) and may lower blood sugar.

Another surprise discovery is for people who suffer from ulcers and have traditionally been advised to avoid spicy foods. New research indicates capsaicin may provide protection against peptic ulcers and may also protect gastric mucosal membranes against damage from alcohol and aspirin.

Chile peppers can even help people lose weight. Recent research indicates that chiles, low in calories and high in potassium, speed up your metabolism and help you burn calories. They also add a lot of flavor without any fat. Chiles also serve as a preservative in frozen or cooked-meat dishes and are an excellent source of vitamins A and C. As the pods ripen and redden, the carotene (vitamin A) and ascorbic acid (vitamin C) increase.

Varieties of Chile Peppers

Today more chile peppers are grown and consumed than any other seasoning ingredient in the world. A common misconception is that all are hot; this is far from the truth. There are hundreds of varieties of chiles with differing flavors and heat levels. Some even have similar names, which adds to the confusion. For example the *chile ancho* is dried poblano. The same chile in California is called *pasilla*. Other problems stem from differences in soil types and climatic conditions. All these variables go into creating a wide range of heat levels.

Dr. Roy Nakayama of New Mexico State University developed the following hotness guide. It lists chile peppers ranging from #1, the lowest or coolest, to #10, the highest or hottest. Here are the top 10 commercially available varieties. I do not include the sensational Bhut Jolokia from Assam, India, because this, the hottest of all chiles, is not yet readily available here in the United States.

10	Bahamian (Habanero)
9	Santaca (Japanese)
8	Tabasco or Serrano
7	Jalapeño
6	Española and Cayenne (hotter)
5	Sandia
4	Hot Ancho
3	Numex Big Jim
2	Rio Grande
1	New Mexico #6, formerly know as Anaheim

Heat can be adjusted in any recipe by using a type of chile higher or lower on the heat scale. New Mexicans want the chile *flavor* not just the heat, although many do seem to have a higher threshold of "pain" than say New Englanders. Believe me, each type of chile has its own distinctive taste. New Mexico recipes often mix chiles, allowing one to enjoy the different taste sensations provided by each alone and in combination. Also, in general red and green chiles differ in flavor. The mature red chile has a richer, warmer flavor than the immature green version of the same chile.

Preparation of Chile Peppers

Whenever possible, use fresh chile peppers. Proper preparation is the key to maintaining the best flavor. Chiles have an outer skin (Mother Nature's cellophane), which must be blistered and charred to separate it from the flesh. Best for roasting chiles is an outdoor barbecue grill.

Because it takes as long to char one chile as it does a dozen or so, you should prepare a batch at a time; a bushel can be done in an hour or so. If you are only roasting a few, you can use your kitchen broiler.

Slit each chile with a small knife to allow steam to escape during the roasting. Turn the chiles as needed, because the entire skin needs to blister. Try not to disturb the flesh underneath. After the chiles are charred evenly, remove them from the grill and place them in a heavy plastic bag. Seal the top of the bag with a twist tie and allow them to sit for at least 20 minutes. As they cool, the internal steam loosens the skin from the flesh. The more delicate varieties, such as the *poblanos*, should be dipped in cold water when taken from the grill to stop the cooking action. Then peel them immediately. An alternate peeling method is the use hot oil to blister the skin. Heat the oil to 275°F (135°C) and place the chiles in the hot oil for one minute or until the chiles are fully blistered. Remove from the oil and peel. They will not have the roasted flavor but are preferred by some people.

Freshly gathered chiles peel quite easily and can be stored in a plastic bag in the refrigerator, where they will stay fresh for up to two weeks. If you plan to freeze the chiles for later use—and they do freeze well—freeze them with charred skin in place. If you plan to use the chiles whole, slit them along the side and carefully remove the inner white veins. A pair of small scissors will do the job. If you plan to puree, strip or chop the chiles, you should remove the stems, seeds and veins.

A word of caution: When dealing with the hotter chile varieties you must not be faint of heart, but it always wise to take a few precautions. The capsaicin oil, the stuff that makes them hot, is primarily located in the seeds and the veins. Contact with them can be painful. Therefore, use rubber gloves during the preparation to protect your hands from "chile burn" and avoid spreading the irritating oil to the eyes, mouth and nose. You also may need to protect your eyes and nose from the vapors, which can cause coughing and sneezing.

Today cooking with chiles can be great fun regardless of where you live. A number of farmers' markets and supermarkets throughout the United States now offer both green and red fresh chiles. They should be used or processed within 3 to 5 days. Dried and packaged chiles keep much longer and are becoming easier to find each year; in fact, they can be ordered by mail anywhere in the United States (See "Where To Buy Chiles," p. 216). Many national chains, such as Whole Foods, are beginning to carry chile products.

Chile vs. Chili

Many people confuse the word "chile" with the word "chili." Chile spelled with an "e" is the vegetable itself. Chili spelled with an "i" is a mixture of spices along with one or more varieties of chile peppers and meat. Sometimes beans are added, but to a real connoisseur, chili is only spices and meat, usually pork. Because of its popularity, I have included a number of chili recipes and an additional collection of dishes that use chili as an ingredient. Wherever I have suggested one of my chili recipes, feel free to substitute your favorite chili, either homemade or canned. There is no question that one of New Mexico's major contributions to American cuisine is chili.

In 1967, a famous chili duel was fought between the late humorist, H. Allen Smith, author of many books and the article *Nobody Knows More About Chili Than I do*, and Wick Fowler. Over a thousand spectators attended this duel, held in the remote town of Terlingua, Texas. This was the start of a national phenomenon, the "chili cookoff." Today, hundreds of service clubs, national organizations and local groups use cookoffs as money-raising events in cities across the country. It is estimated that three quarters of a million people attend these events each year.

"Chilimania" is not, as some might think, a masochistic desire to punish oneself, but rather an influence of today's immigrants with their dynamic population mix. Many of these new Americans come from Mexico, Central America, the Caribbean, Asia or Africa, and they have one thing in common. For centuries, the flavors of their typically bland, inexpensive foods have been enhanced with chile peppers of one kind or another.

CORN

That Amazing Maize

Kernels of corn dating to approximately 360 BC have been discovered in New Mexico's Bat Cave (Carlsbad Caverns) in the southeastern part of the state. According to archaeologists, it was cultivated as early as 217 AD by the Southwest Basketmaker culture. Corn is still considered to be the essence of life by many Pueblo Indians. Believed to have a magical sacredness, it has both religious and symbolic significance to these people. Many tribal ceremonies still call for cornmeal as a prayer offering to the gods. Many Native peoples still scatter cornmeal in their prayer ceremonies to celebrate birth, death, sunrise and sunset.

New Mexico is home to two-dozen varieties of corn, with colors ranging from white to blue and from yellow to bright red. Each of these colors has significance to the Indians. Sweet yellow is eaten roasted on the cob. To make flour, hominy, tamales and bread, white is used. The blue variety is frequently used for tortillas, baking and drinks. Red is used for *piki*, a brittle bread, that was the predecessor of today's tortilla and is still made today by the Hopi.

New Mexico cooks use corn in many ways. Hominy, a dried corn processed with lime in water, is used to make traditional dishes such as *posole*, a favorite New Year's Day good luck dish. Cornmeal is made from the nutritional part of the corn kernel, the endosperm. It can be yellow, white or blue.

Although corn is dried all over the Southwest, in New Mexico these kernels are called *chicos*. They are small and wrinkled in appearance, and, if the corn was roasted before drying, they can be very dark as well. When they are cooked, usually in combination with beans (a handful to a pot), they swell up to their former size and taste like freshly smoked corn. They also can be cooked alone, but as they are very labor intensive to produce, this preparation method is more rare. In this cookbook, I have stayed away from using chicos because this type of corn is so difficult to obtain outside the Southwest.

The tortilla was originally an Aztec invention, which the Spanish found when they came to what is now Mexico. To prepare tortillas, kernels of corn are soaked in water that contains lime to make the skins come off. Then the softened kernels are ground into smooth dough called *masa* and patted into thin round cakes.

Corn's simple carbohydrate structure was the primary leg of the Indian's food triad. Cultivated corn, often processed with wood ash, also provided the Indians with iron and improved their amino-acid balance. They rarely suffered from pellagra, as did many who ate non-corn-based diets.

Because corn required little or no care after planting, the Indians could grow it in an appropriate location, usually on the flat, rich soil near a stream, and return only in the fall to harvest what had survived the animals' and Mother Nature's scourges. This was a great benefit for nomadic tribes: Because the corn was self-sustaining, they were free to roam, hunting for game, berries and plants.

Corn, the primary ingredient of many nations' food chains, today is one of our most important cash crops. The United States produces over half of the world's supply of this versatile, nutritious food.

BEANS
Sustenance from a pod

Many credit the bean for the start of community living in the Southwest. Because beans require more care and tending, the planting of beans meant the end of the nomadic roaming of the Southwest Indians. The bean added complex carbohydrates, which balanced the simple carbohydrates of corn in their diet. This combination, which we now recognize, was critical to survival, as the increasing population of the Southwest made game more scarce. Squash added the third element, oil from its seeds. With corn, beans, squash seeds, piñon nuts, chiles, wild berries and plants, the Indians had the eight essential amino acids necessary for a well-balanced diet. Because beans are high in protein and were relatively easy to grow, they became increasingly important as the supply of buffalo and other game became more limited.

No single food was more important to the development of the West than the bean. From chuckwagon cook to gold miner, homesteader to railroad gandy dancer driving his metal pikes, this little bundle of carbohydrates, protein and fiber was critical. Beans, sustenance in a pod, were to a New Mexican what potatoes were to the Irish, rice to the Chinese, or pasta was to an Italian. It was the staple—cornerstone, if you will—of his diet. With the addition of many different varieties to augment the little speckled brown pinto bean that improves in flavor every time you heat it, today beans are no less important to Southwest cuisine than they were more then 300 years ago. The pinto bean is the most commonly used in New Mexico cuisine; however, other beans are popular. The purple striated Anasazi, my personal favorite, is steadily gaining popularity.

It was common for the Indian farmers to plant corn and squash, then add beans in the same row. As the corn reached a few inches high, the beans would use the corn as beanpoles. The corn plant then shaded the squash. The squash leaves, an ideal ground cover, conserved any valuable moisture that happened along.

There are many schools of thought when it comes to cooking beans. Some soak the dry beans overnight; others say there is no need to pre-soak them at all. Choose whatever method suits you best from the following three options.

If you do not plan to soak the beans overnight, wash 2 cups, remove the debris or broken bad beans and add 8 cups of distilled or purified water. Remove any beans that float to the top. Add 2 tablespoons of bacon grease, oil of choice or lard and 2 cloves of garlic. Bring to a boil in a large kettle and simmer for 3 or 4 hours, adding boiling water as needed. Keep water level slightly higher than the top of the beans. Continue cooking until they are tender. Add a tablespoon of salt before serving.

Soaking beans cuts the cooking time. To soak beans, wash 2 cups and remove any debris, broken or bad beans. Cover with cold water and remove any beans that float to the top. Then let them sit overnight. Drain and rise well. Place in a kettle and add bacon grease, oil or lard. Bring to a boil and cover. Simmer for 1-1/2 to 2 hours or until tender.

I prefer to use a pressure cooker, which is the quickest method of all. I use 2 cups of washed and sorted beans and place 8 cups of distilled or purified water in a pressure cooker. Next I bring water to a gentle boil for about 10 minutes them add the bacon grease. I remove the cooker from the heat, put the lid on and let the beans sit for about 2 hours. One hour before I intend to serve, I add 2 tablespoons of salt then cover the cooker and bring it to 15 pounds of pressure for 12 minutes, after which I remove the cooker from the stove and allow the pressure to drop naturally.

If you regularly have problems cooking beans to the desired tenderness within the specified cooking times, it is probably because your water is hard. High concentrations of minerals in your water will interfere with the chemical and physical changes that are supposed to occur in beans during soaking and cooking. I always use distilled or purified water when I cook or soak beans.

TORTILLAS
The Southwest Bread of Life

No other food product is as versatile as the tortilla. Corn or flour, this staple of most New Mexican cooking is its most important ingredient. With no refrigeration, being able to use dried food during the winter months was critical to the Indians' survival. Corn, because it stores well and is ground quickly, was ideal. It was ground into masa, then formed and shaped by hand into flat, round, thin pancakes. Tortillas were used as food scoops and wrappers for a variety of recipes using chiles, corn and beans.

Today, an endless variety of recipes—tacos, burritos, chimichangas, enchiladas, quesadillas, flautas, tostadas—all depend on these little thin cakes of corn or flour for their existence. Along with red or green sauces, salsa and toppings, they are the heart and soul of New Mexico cuisine.

Making tortillas is an art form and watching someone pat them out and make a nice, neat, flat cylindrical stack is a pleasure. Fortunately, quality tortillas are available in almost every market that offers other bread products. But just in case you wish to make your own tortillas, I have included instructions (See page 55).

A Note to Vegetarians

Our cuisine is basically very simple and easily adapted to the needs of vegetarians, since it uses corn, beans, chiles, squash and nuts. Using canola oil and other healthy substitutes for animal fat such as lard or higher-fat oils easily changes traditional New Mexican foods into meals that meet their nutrimental needs. In many cases, depending on the recipe, meat can be eliminated, since beans, nuts, seeds, chickpeas and corn, important ingredients of our cuisine, are great sources of protein. Also, chiles and dried beans are high in iron, and regular or low-fat dairy products provide their needed calcium.

A message from the author

Over the years I've had the privilege of meeting many fascinating folks who share my love of the Land of Enchantment, and I have been proud to share my knowledge of this unique cuisine with them. I expect you will find, as they have, that once you experience the joyful adventure of New Mexico cooking, most other cuisines will seem bland and unexciting by comparison.

Working on this new cookbook has once again been a pleasure. I have enjoyed every minute of it, and, as I described each recipe, I remembered with pleasure the wonderful folks who shared it with me. I would especially like to thank Nellie Fields, Marge Sanchez, and Yolanda Martinez. All these ladies are cooks of extraordinary talents who have graciously shared their knowledge and recipes. My culinary studies have taught me a great deal about the variety of people who call this beautiful land their home—which is also the homeland of the Native Americans, for whom I have also gained a deep appreciation.

Along with the recipes, I have included a number of "Notes" for your enjoyment. New Mexico has one of the most unique histories and cultures in the United States. I hope you enjoy these little bits of information and learn a little more about this unusual state and its cuisine. In my research I have found these tidbits to be both engaging and appealing, and I wanted to share some of them with you.

It is my belief that there is no such thing as ownership of recipes—they are to be shared and enjoyed. Each must stand on its own. I have done my best to present you with those I consider special in some way or another. I hope you find them as interesting and pleasing to your palate as I have. I personally know each to be worthy of your efforts.

So, what are you waiting for? Head for the kitchen and try them out. Meanwhile, from the Land of Enchantment—Mucho Gusto!

Clyde Casey
Roswell, New Mexico

APPETIZERS

For many years a crisp, fresh tortilla chip dipped in a sassy salsa has been the dominant appetizer of New Mexico. This treat is served as a prelude to a typical meal in almost every restaurant in the Land of Enchantment. For your enjoyment, later in this cookbook (See p. 149), I have included an entire section devoted to salsas. In this chapter are some other appetizers you will enjoy serving.

Please try my Josefinas for your next party. Make sure you fix a large amount, as these treats will be a sure hit. If you add my Corn and Pecan Dip, make sure you have copies of the recipe ready for your guests. I've given away more copies than I can count since I first tasted this dip at an art show in Taos, years ago.

Avocado Dip

One of the problems with avocados, as well as many other fruits, is browning once they are peeled or bruised. The use of lemon juice or chilling below 40°F (4°C) will slow down the enzyme action that causes the browning.

3 medium avocados
2 tablespoons lemon juice
½ teaspoon salt
¼ teaspoon fresh ground black pepper
1 cup dairy sour cream
½ cup mayonnaise
1 ¼-ounce package taco seasoning mix
1 21-ounce can bean dip, plain or jalapeño
1 cup chopped green onions
3 tomatoes, seeded and chopped
1 7-ounce can chopped and pitted olives
2 cups (8 ounces) shredded, sharp Cheddar cheese
tortilla chips

1. In a medium-size bowl, peel, pit and mash avocados. Mix in lemon juice, salt and pepper.
2. In a separate bowl, combine sour cream, mayonnaise and taco seasoning.
3. To assemble, spread bean dip on a large shallow platter.
4. Spoon avocado mixture over bean dip. Top with dairy sour cream and taco mixture.
5. Sprinkle with cropped onions, tomatoes and olives.
6. Cover with shredded cheese. Serve with tortilla chips

Makes about 8 servings.

When shopping for lemons, choose ones with the smoothest skins. They are juicer and have a better flavor. If you submerge a lemon in hot water for 15 minutes before you squeeze it, you will get almost twice the amount of juice. Lemons can be kept for up to a month in your refrigerator if you sprinkle them with water and keep them in a sealed plastic bag.

Bean and Cheddar Dip

A delicious dip sure to be a hit at your next party. If you can find them, substitute white Aztec beans for the pinto beans.

½ cup mayonnaise
1 15-ounce can of pinto beans, drained and mashed
1 cup shredded Cheddar cheese
1 4-ounce can of New Mexico green chiles, drained and chopped
　　OR 3 to 5 fresh or frozen green chiles, roasted, peeled, seeded,
　　de-veined and chopped
¼ teaspoon of your favorite hot sauce

1. Preheat oven top 350°F (175°C).
2. In a glass bowl, stir together all ingredients until well mixed.
3. Spoon into small ovenproof dish.
4. Bake uncovered for 30 minutes or bubbly.

Makes 1½ cups.

In 1821, the Santa Fe Trail was opened by the arrival of Captain William Becknell of Missouri as he led a small string of pack animals into the Santa Fe Plaza. Wagon trains began to roll in with trade goods shortly thereafter. The Santa Fe Trail became an international trade route between the United States and Mexico. After the acquisition of the Southwest, this vital trail helped open up the region to U.S. economic development, playing a critical role in the expansion of the United States into the West. This vital commercial highway served the West until the railroads came into Santa Fe in 1880.

Caramelized Carnitas Burritos

This is an interesting dish that can be offered as an appetizer or as an entrée. *Carnitas* are little pieces of meat, generally pork.

1½ pounds boneless pork shoulder
2 tablespoons packed brown sugar
1 tablespoon tequila
1 tablespoon dark molasses
½ teaspoon salt
¼ teaspoon ground black pepper
2 garlic cloves, minced
½ cup water
½ cup green onions chopped
6 warmed flour tortillas

1. Cut pork into 1-inch cubes. Place in a single layer in a 10-inch skillet.
2. Top with remaining ingredients, except for green onions.
3. Bring to a rolling boil; reduce heat.
4. Simmer uncovered, stirring occasionally, until water has evaporated and pork is slightly caramelized, about 35 minutes.
5. Sprinkle with green onions and serve as filling for warmed tortillas.

Makes 6 servings.

At one time in the early 1900s, British entrepreneur Fred Harvey operated a dozen Harvey Houses here in New Mexico. These establishments featured good eats and smart service and were renowned for fresh pies, hot coffee and an attractive workforce of young women. It is said that 20,000 Harvey girls left the company to marry cowboys and ranchers, which produced 4,000 babies who grew up to be named Fred or Harvey, sometimes both. Will Rogers once said that Fred Harvey and his "Girls" kept the West in food and wives.

Chile Cheese Appetizer

I serve this often and it's always a hit. It's easy to prepare, and you can easily control the heat level by the variety or quantity of chiles you use. Most grocers carry mild, medium or hot canned green chiles.

10 eggs
½ cup flour
1 teaspoon baking powder
¼ teaspoon of salt
½ cup melted butter
2 4-ounce cans New Mexico green chiles, drained and chopped
    OR 6 to 10 fresh or frozen green chiles, roasted, peeled, seeded, de-veined and chopped
1 pint cottage cheese
1 pound of Monterey Jack cheese, shredded

1. In a large bowl, beat eggs slightly, blend in flour, baking powder and salt.
2. Add melted butter, green chiles, cottage cheese and Monterey Jack cheese.
3. Mix just enough to blend. Spread batter evenly in a glass baking dish. Bake at 400°F (205°C) for 15 minutes, then reduce heat to 350°F (175°C) and bake for additional 35–40 minutes more.
4. Remove from oven and cut into bite-sized squares.
Serve on small square crackers or tostados.

Makes 18 servings.

Corn & Pecan Dip

This dip is a must. The secret is to prepare it a day ahead and then store it in the refrigerator overnight. The flavors must be allowed to blend. This dip travels well and is the best dip I have in my collection.

2 8-ounce packages of cream cheese, softened.
¼ cup lime juice
1 tablespoon ground cumin
1 tablespoon ground red chiles
½ teaspoon salt
dash of fresh ground black pepper
1 cup chopped pecans
1 small white onion, diced
1 small can of whole-kernel corn, drained
tortilla chips

1. In a large bowl, combine all ingredients except corn, onions and pecans.
2. Beat until smooth with electric mixer on medium speed.
3. Stir in corn, onions and pecans. Spoon into serving bowl. Cover and refrigerate overnight.

Serve with tortilla chips.

Serves 6.

Fabian Garcia planted New Mexico's first pecan trees in the early 1900s at the New Mexico State University horticulture farm. More pecan trees were planted across the Mesilla Valley in following years, and the first commercial pecan orchard was established by Dean Stahmann, Sr., south of Las Cruces in the 1930s. By 1970, close to 9,000 acres of pecan orchards were established and more pecan trees were being planted. New Mexico is a now major producer of pecans, growing millions of pounds of these nuts per year. New Mexico has no native pecan trees, and all producing pecans are improved varieties. Around Roswell, where I live, we have several large pecan orchards.

Creamy Salsa Dip

Surprisingly good, this is one of the most unusual dip recipes. You can also use low-fat cream cheese to reduce calories.

1 large white onion, chopped
2 large tomatoes, chopped.
2 4-ounce cans New Mexico green chiles, drained and diced
   Or 6-to-10 fresh or frozen New Mexico green chiles, roasted, peeled, seeded and de-veined, diced
1 8-ounce package of cream cheese
¼ cup picante sauce (medium hot)
salt and pepper to taste
tortilla chips

Makes 5 to 6 servings.

1. In a large skillet stir onion and tomatoes together. Over medium heat, sauté until onion is clear.
2. Add green chiles and cream cheese. Stir until smooth.
3. Add picante sauce, salt and pepper to taste.
4. Do not overcook. Serve with tortilla chips.

Makes 6 servings.

Red or Green? This is the most commonly asked question in a New Mexico restaurant. The waiter or waitress is asking which sauce you prefer on your meal. The customer's general response is, "Which is hotter?" Of course you need to trust your own taste buds, but generally red chiles tend to be milder, if both chiles are picked in the same field. This varies wildly from restaurant to restaurant and even from day to day, if the sauce is made from scratch. If you want to be safe, simply ask for your choice "on the side." Then you can test the sauce before you put it on your meal choice.

Guacamole

One of New Mexico's favorite dishes, guacamole can be used as an appetizer, a sauce for meats and main dishes, a dressing for salads or a filling for tortillas. Easily made, it is best when created from fresh ingredients. Healthy and tasty, guacamole is sure to please whenever you serve it.

4 avocados, soft when pressed with thumb
1 lime
2 cloves garlic, minced
½ cup tomato, chopped
½ cup white onion, chopped
2 jalapeños, minced
3 teaspoons cilantro (or to taste), chopped
salt to taste
corn chips

1. Slice avocados in half and scoop out the soft flesh into a medium-size bowl. Mash gently with a fork.

2. Squeeze some of the juice from the lime over the avocado. Add tomato, garlic, onion and jalapeños and stir together.

3. Taste and adjust the seasonings, adding salt, cilantro and more lime juice if needed.

Serve with chips.

Serves 6.

As you pass through the Chihuahuan Desert and Guadalupe Mountains of Southeastern New Mexico—covered by prickly pear, chollas, sotols and agaves—you might never guess there are more than 300 known caves beneath the surface. By far the largest of these is Carlsbad Caverns, one of the most popular tourist destinations in the United States and considered one of the Eight Wonders of the World.

Every year thousands of visitors come to the cave and watch hundreds of thousands of bats swirl out of its opening each evening from April to late October. Carlsbad Cavern itself has several vast underground chambers, up to 250 feet high, filled with amazing ancient limestone formations of many colors and shapes. Once deep inside, you truly feel like you are in a fairyland. One of the great chambers in this cave has room for 14 football fields.

Green Chile con Queso

One of the standard offerings at any get-together. Served hot on a tortilla or with tortilla chips, it is one of the most common appetizers here in New Mexico.

2 tablespoons butter
2 tablespoons finely chopped onion
1 garlic clove, minced
1 tomato, peeled and finely chopped
1 4-ounce can of New Mexico green chiles, drained and diced
    or 3 to 5 fresh or frozen green chiles, roasted, peeled, seeded,
    de-veined and diced
2 cups (8 ounces) grated Cheddar cheese
½ cup evaporated milk
tortilla chips
green or red jalapeño chiles, seeded and sliced.

1. In a double boiler, melt butter.
2. Add onion and garlic; sauté over medium heat.
3. Add tomato and green chiles; mix well.
4. Remove from heat; add milk and cheese.
5. Place over hot water and cook, stirring constantly until cheese is melted.
6. Cover and continue cooking over simmering water until desired thickness.
7. Cool slightly and garnish with sliced green or red jalapeños. Serve with tortilla chips.

Makes about 2 two and ½ cups.

Horchata

Here's a refreshing, cold rice drink that is finding its way into more and more households here in the Land of Enchantment. Partly because rumor has it that it is a cure for a hangover, it is frequently served as a breakfast drink. It's worth the time it takes to prepare; try it for a new taste treat.

1 cup white rice, uncooked
½ cup blanched almonds
½ cinnamon stick
1 teaspoon lime zest
¼ teaspoon vanilla extract
6 cups water
½ cup white sugar

1. Vigorously pulverize rice in a blender or coffee/spice grinder. Grind as smooth as possible.
2. In a bowl, blend together rice, almonds, cinnamon, lime zest, vanilla extract and 3 cups water. Cover and place in refrigerator over night.
3. In the morning add 2 cups water and again blend until smooth.
4. Strain mixture through fine sieve or layered cheesecloth until no gritty particles remain.
5. Add sugar and remaining cup of water.
6. When sugar is dissolved, serve over ice.

Makes 4 servings.

Josefinas

This cheese-topped toast is a sometimes served as an appetizer and sometimes as bread. The taste can be varied by the type of cheese you use. Here again you can pick the heat level by using mild, medium or hot chiles.

1 slender baguette (½ pound size)
1 cup butter, softened
2 4-ounce cans New Mexico green chiles, drained and chopped
    or 6-to-10 fresh or frozen New Mexico green chiles, roasted,
    peeled, seeded and de-veined, chopped
½ cup minced sweet onion such as Vidalia
3 cloves garlic, peeled and minced
1 cup (¼ pound) shredded Monterey Jack cheese

1. Cut baguette into ½-inch pieces and toast in broiler on one side.
2. In a bowl, mix together butter, green chiles, garlic and onion.
3. Spread the chile mixture evenly on untoasted sides of bread.
4. Top with cheese. Broil until cheese melts and is light brown and puffy.

Serve warm.

Makes 8 to 10 servings.

If your French or Italian bread gets hard because of lack of moisture, sprinkle the crust with cold water and put it in your oven at 350°F for about 10 minutes. Remember if your bread gets moldy it should be disposed of. Please throw it out even if only one piece shows signs of mold. Mold sends out little feelers that are invisible to the naked eye.

Mexican Pinwheels

Whenever I go to a potluck or covered dish lunch, I take these. Easy to prepare these little roll-ups are always a hit. A favorite at any party.

1 8-ounce package of cream cheese
1 8-ounce container of dairy sour cream
1 4-ounce can New Mexico green chiles, drained and chopped
    or 3 to 5 fresh or frozen green chiles, roasted, peeled, seeded,
    de-veined and chopped
½ cup green onions, chopped
1 cup Cheddar or colby cheese, shredded
Lawry's seasoning salt to taste
garlic powder to taste
Soft flour tortillas as needed

1. In a bowl mix together all ingredients except tortillas. Spread evenly on tortillas. Roll up and refrigerate 2 to 3 hours.
2. Slice rolls into bite-sized pieces and secure each with toothpick. Keep chilled until serving.

Serves 10 or 12

Cheddar cheese is a hard, pale yellow-to-orange, sharp-tasting cheese. If you prefer a sharp taste, this is the one to use. Colby is similar to Cheddar but is softer, moister and milder. Longhorn is the best know of the Colby cheeses. Colby should not be aged because it dries out quickly. Colby is sometimes mixed with Monterey Jack and called Colby-Jack or Co-Jack.

Pico de Gallo

When you visit a New Mexico restaurant the first thing you will be served is a small dish of this salsa with corn tortilla chips. The name "Pico de Gallo" means "Rooster's Bill" and refers to the way a rooster pecks at his corn. In a restaurant, watch out, because this is traditionally served HOT!

1 tomato chopped
1 white onion chopped
2 jalapenos, seeded and minced
2 cloves garlic, peeled and chopped
½ teaspoon salt or to taste
juice of ½ fresh lime

1. In a glass or non-reactive bowl, combine all ingredients and let stand for at least 1 hour.

Makes about 2 cups.

New Mexico covers an area of 121,000 square miles of diverse terrain. From top to bottom it plunges through six of the seven life zones, from the tundra to the lower Sonoran Desert. The World famous Rio Grande River runs the length of the state, north to south. This vast, geographically complex terrain gives the state one of the most diverse climates in the United States. Our Northern Mountains are cool and wet but our southern deserts are dry and hot.

Prickly Pear Jelly

If Prickly Pear cactus is native to your area, here is a real treat. Pick cactus fruits in the fall when red or purple and fully ripe, then remove the sharp spines. I use bacon tongs for this. Holding the fruit over a flame with the tongs, burn off the spines.

18 to 20 prickly pear fruits
water to cover
small amount of salt-free butter
¾ cup white sugar per cup of juice
¼ teaspoon cinnamon
1 tablespoon lemon juice per cup of juice
box of natural pectin, in case necessary
6 to 8 small jelly jars
paraffin for sealing

1. Cut fruit into chunks
2. In a non-reactive pan, cover pear chunks with water and simmer until fruit turns mushy, about 15 to 20 minutes. Do not drain.
3. Mash with potato masher.
4. Strain mashed pears through a colander lined with an old clean sheet or at least three layers of cheesecloth; do not force.
5. Place juice from the mashing back into the non-reactive pan and bring to a full boil. Keep at rolling boil for 5 minutes, skimming foam from top as it forms (a small amount of butter can be added to help control foam).
6. Add sugar, cinnamon and lemon juice; boil until candy thermometer reeds 222°F. Skim off foam as it forms on top.
7. Test jelly using sheet test (falls from spoon in a sheet, not drops.). If jelly does not sheet, add a box of natural pectin. If jelly sheets well at 222°F, there is not need to add pectin.
8. Pour into hot sterilized jars and seal immediately with paraffin.

Makes 6 to 8 small jelly jars.

Refried Bean Dip

In addition to its use as a side dish with many New Mexican meals, refried beans also can be utilized as an excellent dip. Here is one the best examples of this versatile offering.

2 cups refried beans (See p. 119 or use canned)
1 cup shredded Cheddar cheese
¼ cup green onions, including some tops, chopped
¼ teaspoon salt
2 or 3 teaspoons your favorite taco or hot sauce
tortilla chips

1. In a skillet, mix together refried beans, cheese, onion, salt and taco or hot sauce.
2. Cook uncovered, over low heat, stirring, until thoroughly heated. Serve warm with tortilla chips.

Makes about 3 cups.

The annual Pinto Bean Festival is usually held October each year in Moriarty, New Mexico. The Festival includes a parade, horseshoe pitching contest, a bean sprout contest and the crowning of the Bean Queen—and, of course, there is also a *frijole* cook-off.

Spiced Deviled Eggs

Served as hors d'oeuvres, a side dish, or a holiday party dish, the New Mexico version of this popular treat has real heat added by red chile powder. Not for faint of heart.

6 eggs, hard boiled
¼ cup real mayonnaise
1 teaspoon prepared mustard
1 teaspoon vinegar
¼ teaspoon salt
½ teaspoon ground red chile
paprika

1. Boil eggs 20 minutes, cool and peel.
2. Cut peeled eggs in half lengthwise and carefully remove yolks.
3. Place yolks in a bowl and mash well with a fork.
4. Add mayonnaise, mustard, vinegar, salt and red chile. Mix well.
5. Stuff egg white halves with mixture. Garnish with paprika.

Makes 12 servings.

After you peel your hard-boil eggs, be sure not to place them in cold water. They have a very thin protective membrane that will allow bacteria growth if it has been damaged or removed. To cool your hard-boiled eggs, just cool them to room temperature and then store them in your refrigerator. To store deviled eggs, place the halves together, wrap with tin foil and twist the ends of the foil. Hard-boiled eggs should never be frozen because their taste and texture is altered.

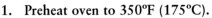

Spicy Hot Pecans

We have three pecan trees in our yard, and this is my favorite way to serve them as a treat or give them as a gift.

½ cup butter
¼ cup Worcestershire Sauce
1 tablespoon garlic powder
1 tablespoon ground red New Mexico chile
1 teaspoon black pepper
2 teaspoons salt
3 cups shelled pecan halves

1. Preheat oven to 350°F (175°C).
2. Melt butter in a pan.
3. Add all ingredients except pecans. Blend well. Remove from stove.
4. Add pecans and stir 3 minutes.
5. Spread on cookie sheet and bake for 15 minutes.

Makes 3 cups.

Hispanic fiestas and feast days are an important part of New Mexico's religious life. Each year during the fourth weekend in July, the small northern village of Chimayo celebrates its fiesta. One of the highlights is the performance of the folk play *Los Moros y Los Cristianos/The Moors and the Christians.*

SALADS, SOUPS & STEWS

Salads on their own are traditionally not a very important part of New Mexico cuisine, and many salads can double as entrees. Years ago, in Questa, New Mexico, I was introduced to the Black Bean Salad. In my version of this zesty salad, I've added corn, which adds to the flavor, color and texture. I also confess to using green chiles rather than bell peppers to pep up my personal version. Jicama with Oranges is another simple salad that offers contrasting textures and flavors. Your health-conscious guests will welcome it. A special treat is Avocado Halves Stuffed with Chicken in Chile Sauce. Many years ago, I was served this delicious salad at the Pink Adobe Restaurant in Santa Fe. Here is my version of this unusual dish.

Hearty soups are an important part of the main meal here; in fact, some can also be served as entrees, Green Chile Potato Soup in particular. Of course we enjoy Anasazi Bean Soup year-round. Posole, a hearty, hominy-based soup, is a must for the holiday season. In some homes the tradition is to serve it Christmas Eve; in others it's New Years Eve. But whenever the weather is chilly, this warming soup is ideal fare. Each household adopts their own version; one of my friends omits the ham hocks and substitutes chicken.

Avocado Halves Stuffed with Chicken in a Chile Sauce

Here's the recipe I mentioned in the introduction to this book. A classic from one of New Mexico's true treasures, the Pink Adobe restaurant in Santa Fe, it is well worth the effort if you want to show off for company.

Salad
3 cups cooked chicken, cut into ½-inch cubes
6 large romaine lettuce leaves
3 ripe avocados, halved, pitted and peeled
1 medium tomato, peeled and cut into wedges
2 hard boiled eggs, peeled and cut into wedges
12 black olives, pitted
2 tablespoons minced fresh chives

Chile Sauce Dressing
1 cup mayonnaise
1 cup bottled chile sauce of choice
1 teaspoon capers
1 teaspoon red chili powder
1 teaspoon chopped pickled jalapeño pepper (or to your taste)
¼ teaspoon salt
¼ teaspoon crushed fresh cilantro

1. In a large bowl, mix all dressing ingredients. Set aside.
2. In another bowl, add dressing a little at a time to cubed chicken using just enough to moisten. Be sure mixture is firm enough to mound into avocado halves.
3. Place a leaf of lettuce on individual plates. Place avocado half one each plate and divide chicken evenly among avocados.
4. Garnish plates with tomatoes, eggs, and olives. Sprinkle the top with chives.

Serves 6.

Some folks consider the avocado a vegetable; however, it is actually a fruit. Beneath its leathery skin is a soft, buttery flesh that yields to light pressure when properly ripe. If you get a hard one, simply set it on the counter for a few days and it will ripen. The flesh has a tendency to discolor rather quickly after peeling. The best way to prevent this is to brush or sprinkle with lemon juice and use as quickly as possible.

Black Bean & Corn Salad

For a change of pace, try substituting your favorite variety of beans. Sometimes I use balsamic vinegar for its pungent sweetness.

2 cups cooked or canned black beans, drained
2 cups cooked or canned kidney beans, drained
2 cups cooked corn kernels
1 green bell pepper, diced
2 green onions, chopped
2 tablespoons vegetable oil
3 tablespoons red-wine vinegar
1 tablespoon honey
¼ tablespoon dry mustard
¼ teaspoon ground cumin
black pepper, to taste

1. In a large serving bowl, combine beans, corn, green pepper, and green onions.
2. In a small jar, stir together oil, vinegar, honey, mustard, cumin and black pepper to taste.
3. Pour over bean mixture. Stir and coat all ingredients.
4. Cover and refrigerate until thoroughly chilled before serving.

Makes 6 servings.

From the time Don Juan de Oñate entered New Mexico in 1598, the building blocks of the state's history have been well-spiced with chile. The Spaniards are said to have brought the vegetable north from the tropical area of the New World; however, evidence is mounting that the ancestors of the Pueblo Indians may have cultivated chiles prior to the Spanish colonization of the Southwest. Regardless, it is clear that chiles played a role not unlike the black pepper of the Old World.

Fiery Potato Salad

Try this excellent example of the versatility of New Mexico cuisine for your next cookout. It is a unique combination of taste and textures that is sure to please.

½ cup extra virgin olive oil
6 tablespoons fresh lime juice
3 large garlic cloves, peeled
2 tablespoons unpeeled jalapeño chiles, chopped and seeded
½ teaspoon ground cumin
1 teaspoon ground Mexican oregano
1 15-ounce can golden hominy, drained
⅔ cup jicama, peeled and diced
½ cup white onion, chopped
¾ cup fresh cilantro, chopped
2 pounds medium-large Yukon Gold potatoes (about 6), unpeeled
salt and fresh ground black pepper

1. In a blender, puree the first 6 ingredients until almost smooth. Season generously with salt. Pour into a medium size bowl. Mix in hominy, jicama, onion and ½ cup of the cilantro. Let stand for 30 minutes.
2. Steam potatoes until tender, about 30 minutes. Cool about 15 minutes, peel. Cut lengthwise in half, then crosswise into ½-inch-thick-slices.
3. In a large bowl, combine potato slices and hominy mixture and toss to blend. Season to taste with salt and fresh ground black pepper.
4. Sprinkle with the remaining chopped cilantro.

Serves 6

Garbanzo Salad

Also known as the chickpea or Indian pea, the garbanzo is a legume that is very high in protein and has a meaty taste that contrasts nicely with the crisp celery and crunchy pecans in this refreshing salad. My wife prefers to use kidney beans, and you might consider trying them instead of the garbanzos.

1 14-ounce can of garbanzo beans, drained
2 cups chopped celery
1 tablespoon minced white onion
½ cup pecans, chopped
2 small sweet pickles, chopped
¼ cup salad oil
3 tablespoons white wine vinegar
½ teaspoon each salt and black pepper
lettuce of choice

1. In a medium bowl, combine garbanzo beans with celery, onion, pecans and pickles.
2. In a separate small bowl, mix oil, vinegar, salt and black pepper.
3. Pour over bean mixture and toss.
Serve on lettuce.

Makes 6 to 8 servings.

New Mexico has numerous hot springs. Among the most famous are the Ojo Caliente Mineral Springs (between Española and Taos) and the Gila Hot Springs (near the Gila Cliff Dwellings on Hwy. 15, outside Silver City). Generations of Native Americans as well as tourists have traveled to the many hot springs located here in the Land of Enchantment to soak and sooth their aches and pains. My father, who had serious health problems, made an annual pilgrimage from Colorado to visit the Montezuma Hot Springs at Las Vegas, New Mexico.

Jicama Salad

An interesting use of the sweet, crunchy, water chestnut-like jicama root, which is humble and uncomely to be sure but delicious to the taste. Try it.

2 cups peeled and diced raw jicama
1 red or green bell pepper, seeded and slivered
½ white onion, medium size, chopped
1 cup diced cucumber
¼ cup extra virgin olive oil
2 tablespoons red wine vinegar
½ teaspoon dried-leaf oregano, crumbled
salt and pepper to taste

1. In a medium-size bowl, combine jicama, bell pepper, onion and cucumber.
2. In another small bowl, mix together oil, vinegar, and oregano. Pour over vegetables and mix lightly. Add salt and pepper to taste.

Makes 4 to 6 servings.

The Jicama is an edible tuberous root. This nondescript vegetable is becoming more popular here in New Mexico. Once you peel away the yellowish, papery skin, the inside is creamy white with a crisp texture that resembles a pear or potato. The jicama has a sweet and starchy taste and is usually eaten raw. Unlike the pear or apple, it does not brown when exposed to the air.

Jicama with Oranges

Sometimes referred to as the "Mexican Potato or Mexican Yam Bean," this sweet, nut-flavored, bulbous root vegetable has a crisp texture. If you have never tasted jicama, here is your chance to enjoy this sweet and crunchy water-chestnut-like root.

6 small navel oranges
1 medium-size jicama
½ cup fresh orange juice
1 red onion, thinly sliced
½ cup cilantro, chopped
1 jalapeño chile, seeded and diced
4 cups mixed salad greens, tossed with vinaigrette
salt and black pepper to taste
chile powder, cayenne pepper or paprika

1. Remove membranes from orange sections. Set aside.
2. With a sharp knife, remove the outer brown peel of the jicama. Rinse in cold water and cut into matchstick-sized pieces
3. In a large bowl, toss orange sections, jicama matchsticks, orange juice, onions, cilantro and jalapeño. Salt and pepper to taste.
4. Cover and refrigerate for about 2 hours.
5. Remove from bowl and drain on paper towel. Sprinkle with chile powder, cayenne or paprika. Serve on a bed of mixed salad greens.

Makes 4 servings.

New Mexico enjoys a relatively low incidence of heart disease. This may be due to the high consumption of red and green chile—an essential part of most New Mexicans' diet. Chiles are believed to help lower cholesterol and promote weight loss. They are also known to improve the immune system and contain vitamin A, which is a potent antioxidant.

Watercress Salad

One of my fondest memories of my youth is my grandmother fixing wilted watercress salad. Watercress was the first green vegetation found on the old family homestead each spring. In those days, no supermarket produce departments were around, so green veggies were scarce in the winter.

2 cups fresh picked watercress
4 or 5 slices bacon
¼ cup apple cider vinegar
3 teaspoons white sugar
⅛ teaspoon ground mustard
⅛ teaspoon red paprika
salt and pepper to taste

1. Thoroughly rinse watercress. Remove any old leaves and thick stems. Set aside in serving bowl.
2. In a small non-stick pan, over medium heat, fry bacon on both sides. Remove bacon from pan and drain on paper towel. Leave bacon fat in pan.
3. Add apple cider vinegar and sugar to bacon fat. Stir to dissolve and bring mixture to simmer.
4. Add ground mustard and paprika and stir.
5. Add salt and pepper to taste.
6. Use as dressing over watercress and toss.

Serves 4

Taco Salad

Everyone loves this salad. A standard for many years, Taco Salad is as popular today as it was 25 years ago. Commercially prepared restaurant-style chips make it an easy-to-prepare treat.

1 pound lean ground beef
1 garlic clove, minced
1 4-ounce can New Mexico green chiles, drained and chopped
    OR 3 to 5 fresh or frozen green chiles, roasted, peeled, seeded,
    de-veined and chopped
1½ cups chopped fresh tomatoes
    Or 1 16-ounce can whole tomatoes, chopped
salt and black pepper to taste
1 cup dairy sour cream
2 tablespoons lemon juice
¼ teaspoon ground cumin
6 cups tortillas, cut in strips and toasted
1 head lettuce, torn into bite-sized pieces
1 cup (4 ounces) grated Cheddar cheese
½ cup chopped green onions, including tops
1 avocado, peeled and sliced

1. In a skillet, brown meat, stirring to break up. Add garlic. Drain on paper towel and return to skillet.
2. Add chiles and tomatoes, with juices if using canned. Add salt and pepper to taste.
3. Cook over low heat for 25 to 30 minutes, adding water if necessary.
4. While meat cooks, prepare dressing. In a small bowl, combine dairy sour cream, lemon juice and cumin. Set aside.
5. Before serving, arrange lettuce, cheese, tortilla strips, and onions in salad bowl.
6. Add meat mixture and toss lightly. Top with dressing and slices of avocado.

Makes 8 servings.

Each year in Albuquerque, the Annual National Fiery Foods and Barbecue Show attracts attendees from around the globe and more than 10,000 visitors. Exhibitors in the show take advantage of the opportunity to meet and greet new buyers, introduce new products and meet the general public, who appreciates fiery food.

Tostadas

The tostadas is the New Mexican version of a chef's salad. Here's the way I like to serve them. Each guest can create their own favorite. The Cotija queso seco is sometimes called the "Mexican Parmesan." It is an aged dry salty cheese with a robust taste that is normally served crumbled over various dishes to enhance flavor.

½ cup high flash or smoke point vegetable oil such as canola or
    peanut
12 corn tortillas
salt
1 cup Refried Beans (See p. 119), heated
1 cup crumbled or grated Cotija Queso Seco (Mexican farmers
    cheese) or a very dry sharp white Cheddar.
1 cup salsa of choice
1 cup thinly sliced iceberg lettuce sprinkled with vinegar and salt
½ cup Guacamole (See page 20)
½ cup sour cream
¼ cup sliced black olives

1. Prepare tortillas: Heat 5 tablespoons of oil in a small skillet on medium high heat until bubbles form immediately when you insert edge of tortilla. Using tongs, place tortilla in hot oil and let cook until golden brown on both sides, about 30 seconds per side. You can use spatula to flatten down tortilla as it cooks. Remove tortilla with tongs and allow excess oil to drip off.
2. Place cooked tortillas on paper towels to absorb more of the oil. Sprinkle a little salt on each tortilla. Store in warm oven until ready for use.
3. To serve, arrange cheese, refried beans, salsa, lettuce, guacamole, sour cream and black olives on serving dishes. Let guests spread the beans and other items as they want on their own tortilla. Keep tortillas and beans warm until ready for use.

Serves 6.

Vegetable, canola, safflower and corn oils have a higher smoke point and a less distinct flavor than olive oil. By combining one of these with your olive oil, you enhance the flavor of the added oil and raise the smoke point of the olive oil. The combination oil is a nice addition to your cooking.

Anasazi Bean Soup

Although new to many people, these colorful beans date back to the ancient, cliff-dwelling Anasazi Indians. Sweeter than pinto beans, they also tend to hold their shape when cooked.

2 cups dried Anasazi beans, cleaned and soaked over night
1 large white onion, diced
2 carrots, peeled and diced
1 large celery stock, finely diced
1 teaspoon dried-leaf oregano
3 garlic cloves, minced
1 teaspoon salt
1 pound fresh tomatoes, peeled, seeded and chopped
2 cups fresh corn kernels
1½ tablespoons soy sauce
1 4-ounce can New Mexico green chiles, drained and chopped
    OR 3 to 5 fresh or frozen green chiles, roasted, seeded, deveined
    and chopped.
small bunch of cilantro

1. Drain beans, cover with fresh distilled or purified water and bring to a boil for 5 minutes. Drain beans again, then cover with 10 more cups distilled or purified water. Add onion, carrots and celery; bring to a boil. Reduce heat, partially cover and simmer for 1 hour.
2. Mash the garlic with the salt and oregano. Add to beans along with the tomatoes and simmer with beans until beans are tender.
3. Add corn, cook until corn is tender. Add soy sauce, chiles, and cilantro.

Makes 6 servings.

Anasazi beans are fast becoming one of America's popular boutique beans. Sometimes called Aztec or Cave beans, they are said to have originated at least 1,500 years ago here in New Mexico. There is a story going around that a member of a team of archeologists, looking for the remains of a Pygmy elephant that once roamed here, found a clay pot sealed with pine tar, and inside it were some of these beans. Carbon dated to over 1,500 years old, some of them actually germinated when planted. True or not these wonderful little purple-red and white beans are my favorite beans.

Mexican Corn Soup

Again we find corn as the main ingredient in a dish. Simple and easy to prepare, this soup is regularly served at lunch or supper in many New Mexico households. One of my personal favorites.

4 cups fresh corn kernels
½ cup white onion, chopped
2 tablespoons butter
2 tablespoons flour
2 cups chicken broth
2 cups milk or cream
1 cup grated Cheddar cheese
1 4-ounce can New Mexico green chiles, drained and chopped
    OR 3 to 5 fresh or frozen green chiles, roasted, peeled, seeded, de-veined and chopped.
½ cup crisp, fried bacon, crumbled
tortilla chips, crumbled

1. In a skillet, over medium heat, sauté corn and onion in butter until onion is soft.
2. Stir in flour and gradually add broth and milk. Stir until thickened. Do not let boil.
3. Stir in cheese and green chiles. Cook until cheese melts.
Top individual servings with crumbled tortilla chips and bacon.

Serves 4 to 6.

The Institute of American Indian Arts Museum is located in Santa Fe. It features the National Collection of Contemporary Indian Art. This permanent collection includes works by prominent artists such as Earl Bliss, T.C. Cannon, Darren Virgil Gray, Fritz Scholder, Doug Hyde, Allen Houser, Charles Loloma and Kevin Red Star.

Chuckwagon Soup

I love the taste and texture of barley. If barley is not your thing you can substitute finely chopped potatoes. Barley was used as animal food here in the west but it was a common practice for the old chuckwagon cooks to toss it into soup and you should give it a try.

2 tablespoons oil of choice
2 pounds ground chuck
1 onion, peeled and diced
4 ribs of celery, diced
2 or 3 carrots, diced
1 green bell pepper, diced
2 large cans (approximately 1 pound, 14 ounces) tomatoes, chopped
3 cups chicken or beef stock
2 4-ounce cans New Mexico green chiles, drained and chopped
    OR 6 to 10 fresh or frozen green chiles, roasted, peeled, seeded,
    de-veined and chopped
¼ teaspoon salt
½ teaspoon fresh ground black pepper
1 cup barley, uncooked
½ teaspoon dried leaf oregano
½ teaspoon basil
½ teaspoon thyme

1. In a 6 quart Dutch oven or heavy pot, brown beef. Add onions, celery, carrots and bell peppers; cook until soft. Drain well and return to pot.
2. Add remaining ingredients to pot and bring to a simmer, then reduce to medium heat. Allow to simmer for at least an hour, stirring occasionally, until barley is somewhat fluffy.

Makes 6 to 8 servings.

Gazpacho Soup

A summertime soup that is sure to please. Served chilled, it is healthy, sophisticated and delicious. The secret is to refrigerate it at least 4 hours before serving.

1 large white onion, peeled and quartered
4 cloves garlic, minced
2 green bell peppers, seeded and quartered.
8 tomatoes, seeded and quartered
1 large cucumber, peeled, seeded and quartered
½ cup green onions with tops, chopped
½ cup lemon juice
2 cups tomato juice
⅓ cup olive oil
2 teaspoons salt
½ teaspoon black pepper
1 cup white wine

Toppings
4 hard-boiled eggs, diced
1 cup croutons
1 red bell pepper, seeded and diced
½ cucumber, seeded and diced
½ cup chives

1. In a blender, puree first eight ingredients. Remove from blender and put in very large bowl. Add remaining ingredients to the bowl and stir well. Cover and store in refrigerator for at least 4 hours. Overnight is even better, as the flavor improves with age.
2. Serve in individual bowls. Place toppings in small serving dishes and allow guests to serve themselves.

Makes 6 servings.

During summer evenings here in New Mexico, enjoying a gazpacho soup in an outdoor restaurant is very popular. What makes this soup so good is the fresh taste of all the vegetables. It's best in the summer when the vegetables are fresh and the most flavorful. People who have never tried a cold soup are sometimes hesitant to try gazpacho but soon become fans of the bright, intense flavors. Gazpacho is one of summer's pleasures!

Green Chile Potato Soup

I love potato soup. My mother used to fix potato soup in the winter, and I never got tired of it. Here in New Mexico the chile peppers give it a warm flavor that adds a new dimension to this old Irish favorite.

3 tablespoons butter
8 green onions, chopped
2 tablespoons all-purpose flour
4 cups milk, heated
1 4-ounce can New Mexico green chiles
    Or 3 to 5 fresh or frozen roasted, peeled, seeded and de-veined
    green chiles, diced
3 medium potatoes, peeled and diced
salt and black pepper to taste
1 jalapeño or serrano chile pepper, seeded and minced
1 cup grated Monterey Jack cheese

1. In a soup pot, heat butter and sauté onions.
2. When onions are soft, stir in flour, slowly stir in heated milk. Stir constantly until mixture begins to boil.
3. Reduce heat to low and add chiles and potatoes; salt and pepper to taste.
4. Simmer 10 minutes or until potatoes are tender.
5. Scoop out 1 cup and puree in blender or food processor.
6. Add puree back to pot and add jalapeño or serrano chiles. Cook 5 minutes more.

Serve with cheese sprinkled on top.

Makes 4 servings.

Available all year, your choice of a potato should be smooth, well shaped and unbruised. Don't buy if it has sprouted or has a green tint to the skin. Store at room temperature in a dark area. Do not refrigerate.

Green Chile Venison Stew

Here is a traditional soup/stew that can be made with any domestic or wild game meat. It provides a full meal in itself and one that you can easily adapt to your own style and taste. Venison is particularly good in this recipe.

4 or 5 strips bacon
1 pound cubed venison
5 cloves garlic, diced
1 can stale beer
4 bay leaves
¼ teaspoon vinegar
½ teaspoon ground cumin
1 tablespoon dried-leaf oregano
3 potatoes, peeled and cubed
1 teaspoon sugar
2 4-ounce cans New Mexico green chiles drained and chopped
    Or 6 to10 fresh or frozen New Mexico green chiles, roasted, seeded, de-veined and chopped.

1. In a heavy pan, fry bacon strips until crisp. Remove and reserve to make bacon bits. Toss venison cubes in flour and add, a few at a time, to brown in bacon fat.
2. Push venison to side and add garlic and onions. Sauté until onions are soft and lightly browned.
3. Add beer, bay leaves, vinegar, cumin and oregano. Cover with water. Simmer until meat is tender, approximately an hour and a half. Add water as needed.
4. Add potatoes, sugar, salt and pepper to taste.
5. When potatoes are tender, add green chiles and simmer a few more minutes.
Serve in bowls garnished with bacon bits.

Serves 6.

Lately, venison has enjoyed new popularity because of its lower fat content. Here in New Mexico, many families use it as a one-on-one substitute for beef.

New Mexico Pinto Bean Soup

This excellent soup is a good example of the use of pinto beans in everyday cooking here in New Mexico. These days your local grocery store should stock the pinto beans in bulk. Check my introduction for detailed instructions for cooking beans (See p. 8).

3 cups dried pinto beans
2 quarts distilled or purified water
1 cup cubed salt pork
3 garlic cloves
½ onion, chopped
2 cups fresh cilantro, minced
1 4-ounce can New Mexico green chiles, chopped
    Or 3 to 5 fresh or frozen, roasted, peeled, de-veined and seeded
    green chiles, chopped
4 cups whole canned tomatoes
salt and black pepper to taste

1. Rinse and sort beans, removing any debris and broken beans.
2. In a large pot, heat water. Add beans, salt pork and garlic.
3. Cover and simmer for 2 hours.
4. Add onion, cilantro, chile peppers and tomatoes. Cover and simmer for ? hours or until beans are tender. Season to taste with salt and black pepper.

Makes 8 servings.

In New Mexico, the pinto bean is an important part of our regional identity. Known here as a *frijol*, the prepared beans are commonly called *frijoles*, or "Cowboy Beans." Pintos can be stored in an airtight container for up to a year. Don't buy if they are cracked or off color. They should have a bright uniform spotted color. After cooking, they can be stored frozen for up to 6 months but only 4 to 6 days in the refrigerator.

Posole

Posole is an old traditional dish customarily served on Christmas Eve. It has many variations. True traditionalists use posole corn. It is difficult to find here, so I use hominy, a softer, blander type of processed corn that is readily available. Posole corn's flavor is more intense and earthy and its consistency is more robust.

4 8-ounce cans hominy
1 pound fresh ham hock
1 pound spare ribs
1 white onion, chopped
1 garlic clove, minced
1 teaspoon dried-leaf oregano
¼ teaspoon ground cumin
1 4-ounce can New Mexican green chiles, chopped
  Or 3 to 5 fresh or frozen, roasted, peeled, seeded and de-veined green chiles, chopped.
salt and black pepper to taste

1. Rinse and drain hominy and place in a large pot; cover with cold water. Boil for 1 hour, adding hot water as needed
2. In another large pot, place ham and spare ribs. Cover with cold water. Bring to a full boil. Remove from heat. Skim and drain, reserving liquid. Rinse remaining meat with cold water.
3. Add meat to hominy. Add onion, garlic, oregano and cumin. Cover with reserved liquid.
4. Cook over medium heat about 4 hours or until meat is tender.
5. Add chiles, salt and pepper to taste. Simmer for additional 30 minutes.

Makes 6 servings.

Some folks like to garnish their posole with chopped fresh cilantro, sliced radishes, chopped green onions or a slice of avocado.

Pumpkin Soup

This economical treat for the whole family is my favorite fall soup. With so many new varieties of pumpkins available today, I love to try different ones with this basic recipe.

1 medium pumpkin (about 4 pounds)
1 cup heavy cream
3 cups chicken stock
3 tablespoons light brown sugar
1 teaspoon ground cumin
½ teaspoon ground red chile powder
½ teaspoon ground coriander
⅛ teaspoon fresh ground nutmeg
¾ cup grated sharp Cheddar cheese
½ cup chopped cilantro for garnish
salt to taste

1. Preheat oven to 375°F (190°C).
2. Halve the pumpkin, from the top down. Scoop out the seeds and place cut side down on an oiled baking sheet. Bake until pumpkin can be easily skewered, about 45 to 60 minutes. Remove from oven and allow to cool for about 15 minutes.
3. Scrape the pulp and reserve. Discard the skin.
4. In a heavy, medium pot, bring the cream and chicken stock to a boil. Whisk in reserved pumpkin pulp, brown sugar, cumin, chile powder, coriander and nutmeg. Reduce heat to medium and simmer until soup thickens and flavors blend. This should take about 15 minutes. Add salt and pepper to taste.
5. Ladle soup into bowls and garnish with cheese and cilantro.

Serves 6.

Tortilla Soup

Here's a good way to use up your old dried-out corn tortillas. It's quick and easy to prepare.

1 package of corn tortillas
peanut oil or oil of choice for frying
3 medium white onions chopped
3 14-ounce cans of chicken broth
2 8-ounce cans of tomato sauce
1 16-ounce can of diced tomatoes
1 4-ounce can diced New Mexico green chiles
1 garlic clove, finely chopped
1 tablespoon fresh lime juice
½ cup chopped cilantro
3 cups grated Monterey Jack cheese
Salt to taste

1. If you have started with dried-out corn tortillas, great. If you haven't, you will need to dry your fresh tortillas. Lay them on a baking sheet then place them in your oven at 200°F (93°C) for 10 to 15 minutes.
2. Cut tortillas in half and then cut halves into ¼-inch strips. In a 3-quart saucepan, heat oil over medium high heat. Fry strips in oil ⅓ at a time, until brown and crisp. Remove from pan and drain on paper towels. Reserve.
3. Add chopped onions to same sauce pan and sauté over medium-low heat until soft, about 5 minutes. Add broth, tomato sauce, diced tomatoes, chiles and garlic; simmer 20 minutes. Add lime juice.
4. To serve, divide half of the tortilla strips and place equally in the bottom of 6 serving bowls.
5. Ladle soup into each bowl and top with cheese and remaining tortilla strips. Garnish with cilantro.

Serves

Two-Pepper Soup

Another New Mexico soup that is warm and soothing on a cold day. Roasted peppers add a very appealing taste. Substitute red or yellow bell peppers if available and you add another enjoyable flavor.

3 green bell peppers
1 4-ounce can New Mexico green chiles, chopped
    OR 3 to 5 fresh or frozen, roasted, peeled, seeded and de-veined
    green chiles, chopped.
1 small white onion
4 cups chicken broth
2 tablespoons butter
2 tablespoons all-purpose flour
1 cup cream or evaporated milk
salt and black pepper to taste
dairy sour cream

1. Rinse bell peppers and cut off stems. Place in large pan of boiling water. Cover and cook for about 5 minutes Drain, peel, remove seeds and veins, and cut into quarters.
2. Puree bell peppers, chiles and onion in a food processor or blender with one cup of chicken broth.
3. In a large saucepan, melt butter and blend in flour. Gradually stir in chile mixture and remaining chicken broth. Bring to a boil; reduce heat and simmer gently, constantly stirring, until soup is smooth. Blend in cream or undiluted evaporated milk. Heat through. DO NOT BOIL. Season with salt and pepper to taste. Top with a dollop of sour cream.

Makes 6 servings.

Mesilla is a small town located two miles south of Las Cruces, New Mexico, on a little piece of land that rises above the Rio Grande River. Settled in 1850, this farming community is the heart of New Mexico chile-growing activities. It is also the home of the famous La Posta restaurant, founded in 1939. Across from the Mesilla Plaza, the historic building in which the restaurant is located is very interesting. While inside, you can visit the indoor patio with its plants and birds and enjoy a great meal.

BREADS

Tortillas are served as bread in most New Mexico homes. Until recently corn tortillas were used almost exclusively, but flour tortillas are now becoming more and more the bread of choice. I have included recipes for both the corn and flour tortillas, if you decide to make them. Also I have included a recipe for Sopapillas. The Sopapilla is a bread unique to New Mexico; it is very different from the Latin American Sopapilla. The New Mexico Sopapilla is a pillow puff of fried pastry and the Latin American is a type of tortilla.

Here you will also find selected specialty breads for your enjoyment. I would like to call your attention to Navajo Fry Bread. This bread is very simple and delicious served hot with honey or powdered sugar. I have watched Indian women make and fry these breads at powwows and arts and craft shows. I'm always amazed at how easily they take a ball of dough and, with a few quick patting and pulling motions, create a round flat shape ready for frying. This bread is a welcome addition to any meal. Try it with Indian Tacos (See p. 96).

Muffins are a frequent choice here in the Land of Enchantment and I've included three different recipes. Be sure to try the Jalapeño Corn Muffins, courtesy of Chef Jeff Pufal of the Pecos River Learning Center. You have never tasted any muffins like these. Blue corn is another ingredient that we've learned to enjoy since moving here to New Mexico. It's gaining popularity across the country as distribution improves. My Blue Corn Maple Muffins and Blue Cornbread are nice introductions to its unique flavor.

TORTILLAS
The Southwest Bread of Life

The tortilla is the mainstay of New Mexican cooking. Corn Tortillas are fried until crisp and can be stacked, rolled, folded, torn or cut and crumbled, making them among the most versatile of breads. Flour tortillas are served as bread in a steamy hot form, often in a moist napkin or insulated container to keep them as warm and soft as possible. You can find corn or flour tortillas (fresh or frozen) in most supermarkets, but here is some information in case you would like to try making your own.

Be forewarned, if you have never tried making your own tortillas, this process is an art. Corn Tortillas are made from *masa harina*, a Mexican dough derived from corn treated in a solution of lime and water then dried. Regular cornmeal cannot be substituted. Pat or roll the reconstituted masa into a circular shape—usually about 6 inches in diameter—and trim until evenly round. To make this process easier, you might consider a tortilla press, which is easy to use and inexpensive. It shapes and cuts the tortillas for you.

Flour tortillas can also be made in your kitchen. Use all-purpose flour dough and a rolling pin to flatten. They are generally slightly larger (about 8 inches in diameter) than the corn variety.

Frozen tortillas have a long life and should be thawed before re-heating. Those that aren't frozen should be stored in the refrigerator and covered in order to retain their flavor and keep from drying out.

To reheat flour tortillas, rub each side with a damp hand before heating then place on an ungreased surface. Heat until warm and pliable. Wrapping in a damp towel and heating in a microwave for 20 seconds will also soften the tortilla. Keep tortillas soft by keeping them wrapped in a damp towel or inside a plastic bag.

Corn Tortillas

2 cups masa harina flour
1½ cups warm water

1. Mix masa with enough warm water to make dough hold together.
2. Shape dough with your hands into a smooth ball. Divide dough into 12 equal pieces and shape each piece into a ball.
3. If you have a tortilla press, place each dough ball on a piece of wax paper and hand press slightly. Then place a second piece of wax paper on top. Place the wax paper-covered dough in the press and push down. Repeat for each tortilla. Stack, cover and refrigerate until ready for cooking.
4. If you use a rolling pin, place dough ball between two pieces of cloth that have been dipped in water and rung out. Roll ball of dough out with light, even strokes, turning until shape is a circle, about 6 inches in diameter. Carefully pull back the cloth and trim the dough to a round circle, if necessary. Repeat for each tortilla. Stack, cover and refrigerate until ready for cooking.
5. Place tortilla on a dry, heavy griddle or frying pan that has been preheated over medium heat to approximately 350°C (175°C).
6. Cook until dry around the edge, about 1½ minutes. Turn over and repeat process until tortilla is dry, about 2 minutes. Flatten with a spatula if necessary.
7. Stack tortillas, placing wax paper between each, then cover with a damp towel.
8. May be served hot or wrapped in foil and stored in refrigerator.

Makes 12 Corn Tortillas

Flour Tortillas

3 cups all-purpose flour.
2 teaspoons baking powder
¾ teaspoon salt
About 1 cup warm water
3 tablespoons lard or shortening

1. Sift together flour, baking powder and salt. Cut in lard or shortening until particles are the size of fine crumbs. Gradually stir in enough water until flour is moistened and dough almost cleans the side of the bowl.
2. Turn out on a lightly floured board. Knead until smooth.
3. Divide into 12 pieces and roll each into a ball. Cover with plastic film and let rest for 20 minutes.
4. Flatten each ball into a 4 or 5 inch patty. Using a rolling pin, roll each patty from the center to the edges, making a thin circle. Turn dough often.
5. As each tortilla is shaped, place it on a dry, heavy griddle or frying pan that has been preheated over medium heat to approximately 350°C (175°C).
6. Almost immediately little blisters will appear. Turn tortilla and press down gently but firmly with a broad spatula. When blisters form over most of the surface turn over and repeat process, pressing until blisters are light brown. Tortilla should be soft. If tortilla sticks or browns too quickly, reduce heat.
7. Stack tortillas inside a folded cloth towel inside a plastic bag and let steam until all are cooked. They may be served hot or wrapped in foil or a plastic bag and stored in refrigerator.

Makes 12 Flour Tortillas.

Apple Crunch Muffins

My favorite muffin. As soon as the new crop of green apples is available, we make these delicious muffins. The Nut Crunch Topping is quick and easy special treat.

Muffins
1½ cups unbleached flour, sifted.
½ cup sugar
2 teaspoons baking powder
½ teaspoon salt
1½ teaspoons ground cinnamon
¼ cup vegetable shortening
1 large egg, slightly beaten
½ cup milk
1 cup unpeeled tart apples, cored and grated
Nut Crunch Topping

Nut Crunch Topping

1¼ cups packed brown sugar
¼ cup chopped pecans
½ teaspoon ground cinnamon
In a small bowl, mix together sugar, pecans and cinnamon.

1. Preheat oven to 375° (190°C). Place paper liners in muffin-pan cups.
2. Sift together flour, sugar, baking powder, salt and cinnamon into a medium-size bowl. Cut in shortening with pastry blender until fine crumbs form.
3. Combine egg and milk. Add dry ingredients all at once, stirring just enough to moisten. Stir in apples.
4. Spoon batter into prepared muffin-pan cups, filling two-thirds full.
5. Prepare Nut Crunch Topping, mixing together the sugar, pecans and cinnamon. Sprinkle over muffins.
Bake in preheated oven 25 minutes or until golden brown. Serve with butter and jelly or jam.

Makes 12 muffins

Blue Corn Maple Muffins

Blue corn has always been the ritual grain in New Mexico. Blue corn often is higher in lysine and protein than yellow corn. Lysine is an essential amino acid necessary for building protein in our bodies. These muffins make a perfect introduction to this unique corn's flavor.

¼ cup melted butter
⅓ cup maple syrup
1 cup milk
1 egg, beaten
1 cup roasted blue corn meal
1 cup unbleached flour
3 teaspoons baking powder
¼ teaspoon salt

1. Preheat oven to 425°F (220°C). Generously grease muffin pan.
2. Combine melted butter with maple syrup and milk in a small bowl.
3. Beat egg until smooth. In a separate bowl, stir together corn meal, flour, baking powder and salt.
4. Gently combine liquid ingredients with dry ingredients.
5. Spoon batter into prepared muffin-pan cups, filling ¾ full.
Bake about 15 to 20 minutes or until lightly browned.

Makes 12 muffins.

One of the most unique varieties of corn found here in New Mexico is blue corn. During Coronado's 1540 expedition into the Southwest, he found blue corn and other flour corns to be the major staple of the Pueblo Indians. Most blue corns grown here are flour corns. A hard shell that contains a blue pigment gives the corn its blue color. This shell protects covers the soft, floury endosperm. Blue corn has less starch and a lower glycemic index (GI) than yellow corn, which is good news for dieters and people with diabetes.

Blue Cornbread

Here is a traditional New Mexico bread that uses blue cornmeal. You may use yellow or white cornmeal, but the cornbread will not have the same taste and texture that you'll get from blue corn.

1½ cups blue cornmeal
2 teaspoons baking powder
3 tablespoons sugar
¾ cup milk
1 egg, beaten
3 tablespoons melted butter, bacon fat or oil
¼ cup crumbled cooked bacon
1 4-ounce can New Mexico green chiles, drained and chopped
    OR 3 to 5 fresh or frozen green chiles, roasted, peeled, seeded,
    de-veined and chopped.

1. Preheat oven to 350°F (175°C). Generously grease an 8-inch-square pan.
2. In a small bowl, combine cornmeal and baking powder.
3. In another small bowl, mix the remaining ingredients. Combine the ingredients of both bowls and mix. Mixture should be moist.
Pour into prepared pan and bake 30 minutes, or until done.

Makes 6 servings.

New Mexico's culture has had a major influence on cornbread. The state's contributions include cornbread made with blue corn, jalapeño peppers, green chile and varieties of other peppers. These unique types of cornbread changed this once mundane food into a gourmet treat. Cornbread is cheap and easy to prepare and very nutritious.

Chuckwagon Bread

Also known as Sourdough Bread, this is made without adding yeast, but it requires you to make a starter. Here are the few simple steps required to make this bread as folks have been making it for thousands of years. I find its unique taste is worth the effort.

Sourdough Starter
1½ ounce package commercial dry sourdough starter
2 cups bread flour
2 cups warm water
pinch of active dry yeast

1. In a crock or plastic container, whisk together sourdough starter, flour, pinch of yeast and water. Wisk until smooth and then stretch a few layers of cheesecloth over the top and secure with a rubber band. Let mixture stand at room temperature for 24 hours, stirring it two or three times.
2. After 24 hours you should feed your starter by adding ½ cup of flour and ½ cup warm water.
3. Continue feeding with flour and warm water each 24 hours for 3 or 4 days and your starter is ready to use.

Sourdough Bead
2 cups of starter
2 tablespoons of olive oil or softened margarine
4 teaspoons of sugar
3 teaspoons of salt
3 cups unbleached flour

1. In a large bowl, mix together starter, sugar, salt and oil. Knead in enough flour, ½ cup at a time, to make a good, flexible bread dough. Let dough rise in a warm place, with a damp cloth covering the bowl. Note that sourdough dough rises slower than regular bread dough. Let the dough double in size. If when you poke your finger in the top of dough, it creates a pit that does not spring back, the dough is read to bake.

2. Punch down the dough and knead it a little more. Make a loaf and place it on an ungreased baking sheet that has been lightly sprinkled with salt. Cover with a paper towel and place in warm place to rise again.

3. Place pan with loaf in oven and turn on oven to 350°F (175°C) and bake for 35 to 45 minutes. Do not preheat. Loaf is done when crust is brown and bottom sounds hollow when tapped with a wooden spoon. Place loaf on a cooling rack and let it cool for 1 hour before slicing.

Jalapeño Corn Muffins

If you have never eaten a corn muffin, try this one from Jeff Pufal of the Pecos River Learning Center. I would hate to choose between these wonderful muffins and Mexican Corn Bread (See p. 65).

2 tablespoons shortening
¼ cup butter, softened
¼ cup sugar
2 large eggs
¼ cup buttermilk
2 tablespoons minced jalapeño peppers
½ cup kernel corn
½ cup grated Monterey Jack cheese
½ cup grated Cheddar cheese
½ cup all-purpose flour
½ cup yellow or white cornmeal
1 teaspoon baking powder
½ teaspoon salt

1. Preheat oven to 375°F (190°C). Generously grease 8-inch muffin pan.
2. In a medium-size bowl, cream shortening, butter and sugar until smooth.
3. In a separate bowl, whisk the eggs and buttermilk together.
4. Slowly add the egg and milk mixture to the creamed butter mixture; continue to mix until combined well.
5. Add jalapeño pepper, corn, and cheeses; mix well.
6. In a separate bowl, combine the flour, cornmeal, baking powder and salt.
7. Slowly add the dry ingredients to the wet ingredients and blend together well.
8. Pour into prepared muffin pans, filling to ¾ full. Bake in preheated oven about 18 minutes.

Serve warm with butter.

Make 10 to 12 muffins.

Mexican Cornbread

Cornbread can be served with almost any meal. This cornbread recipe has been around for many years and is one of the best I ever tried. I have to have honey with my cornbread.

1 cup yellow cornmeal
1 cup sifted all-purpose flour
2 tablespoons sugar
4 teaspoons baking powder
½ teaspoon salt
1 large egg
1 cup buttermilk
⅓ cup sour cream
¼ cup vegetable oil
2 or 3 jalapeño peppers, seeded, de-veined and
    chopped

1. Preheat oven to 425°F (220°C).
2. Grease an 8-inch square pan, cast iron skillet or cornbread mold.
3. In a medium bowl, combine cornmeal, flour, sugar, baking powder and salt.
4. To dry mixture, add egg, buttermilk, sour cream, oil and jalapeños. Mix until smooth.
5. Pour into prepared pan. Bake for 20 to 25 minutes or until golden brown.

Serves 6.

Twenty-six miles northeast of Santa Fe is the historic Santuario de Chimayo. Close to 30,000 people come to visit this holy shrine each year, many seeking cures for their ailments or praying for loved ones. Each year, about 2,000 make a pilgrimage there during Holy Week, many arriving on foot from surrounding communities, including Santa Fe. It is believed that dirt from the floor of the chapel possesses healing powers bestowed on it by God. Many claim to have been cured there of diseases, infirmities and unhappiness. In fact, the walls are hung with discarded crutches and before-and-after photographs of healed individuals.

Navajo Fry Bread

Traditional and still popular, this old recipe remains unchanged year after year. At New Mexico fairs, craft shows and Indian powwows, you'll see long lines of people waiting to get their hot fry bread. Folklore tells us that poking a hole in the center lets out evil sprits.

2 cups all-purpose flour
2 teaspoons baking powder
1 teaspoon salt
2 tablespoons shortening
⅔ cup lukewarm water
vegetable oil for frying
jam, honey or powdered sugar

1. In a medium-size bowl, combine flour, baking powder, and salt; cut in shortening until mixture has the appearance of fine crumbs. Sprinkle in water, 1 tablespoon at a time. Use a fork to toss until flour is moistened and dough almost cleans side of bowl. Dough should be soft, but not sticky.
2. On a lightly floured surface, knead dough until smooth. Form into ball, cover and refrigerate for 30 minutes.
3. Heat oil in large skillet to 400°F (205°C). Tear off a piece of dough about the size of a peach. Pat and stretch until thin and round, about 6 to 8 inches in diameter.
4. Poke a hole through the middle and drop into sizzling vegetable oil.
5. Fry circles, turning once, until golden brown, about 1 minute per side. Bread will puff beautifully.

Serve with jam, honey or powdered sugar.

Makes 4 servings.

Near Santa Rosa, New Mexico, is the "Blue Hole," an 81-foot deep artesian well bordered by a ring of sandstone. With a constant temperature of 61°F, this well serves as a dive-training and recreational site for deepwater divers, who come from all over the country year round to enjoy its clear, azure blue water.

New Mexican Spoon Bread

The first time I ate this bread, sometimes also called Chuckwagon bread, was at a chuckwagon supper, where before guests were served, they watched this bread being baked in old cast-iron Dutch ovens over a bed of wood coals. A delicious bread to serve the next time you barbecue!

1 17-ounce can of cream-style corn
¾ cup milk
⅓ cup melted shortening
1½ cups white cornmeal
2 eggs, slightly beaten
½ teaspoon baking soda
1 teaspoon baking powder
1 teaspoon salt
1 4-ounce can New Mexico green chiles, drained and chopped
    or 3 to 5 fresh or frozen green chiles, roasted, peeled, de-veined
    and chopped
1½ cups Monterey Jack cheese

1. Preheat oven to 375°F (190°C). In a large bowl, combine all ingredients except chiles and cheese.
2. Pour one half of batter into a greased 9-inch square pan. Sprinkle ½ of the chiles and cheese on top of the batter. Add remaining batter evenly and top with remaining chiles and cheese.
3. Bake for 45 minutes, or until firm around the edges and slightly soft in the center. To serve, spoon from pan onto plates. Bread is soft, a little firmer than pudding.

Makes 6 servings.

Roswell, New Mexico, is now my home and famous for the "Roswell Incident." The story goes that on July 8, 1947, an alien craft crashed near here, and a press release was issued by the Roswell Army Airfield stating it had recovered a crashed "flying disc." The press release was later retracted and the controversy began. All these years later, the story is still the subject of intense speculation, rumor and questioning, with widely divergent views and passionate debate about what actually happened.

Sopapillas

here over 200 years ago, sopapillas are an important
Mexico cuisine. When made sweet, they are often
drizzled with honey or anise syrup; sometimes they are rolled in
cinnamon and sugar and eaten as a desert. When made larger and
savory, they are filled with ground beef, beans and other ingredients.
They should always be eaten hot, as they tend to be greasy and heavy
when cold. Whether eaten as a desert or a bread, these puffy pillows
of pleasure are easy to fix.

1 package of dry yeast
¼ cup lukewarm water
¾ cup milk
6 tablespoons sugar
1 teaspoon salt
2 tablespoons butter
1 egg, beaten
3 cups flour
honey
approximately 2 inches cooking oil

1. In a small bowl, soften yeast in lukewarm water. Set aside.
2. In a one-quart saucepan, combine milk, sugar and salt. Bring to
   a boil. Remove from heat. Stir in butter. Allow to cool to lukewarm.
3. In a large bowl, combine beaten egg and yeast mixture
   Gradually add flour. Work with hands, if mixture becomes to
   thick to stir. Cover dough with damp cloth and allow to rise
   until doubled in size, about 1½ hours.
4. Punch down; turn out onto a lightly floured board and knead
   briefly until dough is smooth.
5. Cover dough and let it rest for an additional 15 minutes. Roll it
   to about a ½ inch-thick-square and cut it into triangular or
   rectangular shapes.

6. Heat oil to 350°F (175°C). Cook sopapillas a few at a time, browning on one side and turning only once. They will puff up.
7. Drain on absorbent paper towels and serve. Most New Mexicans bite off one end and dribble honey inside.

Makes 8 to 10.

ıcchini Nut Bread

ead, Zucchini Nut Bread is deliciously moist

ɔ eggs
2 cups sugar
3 teaspoons vanilla extract
1 cup vegetable oil
2 cups grated, unpeeled zucchini
2 cups all-purpose flour
1 cup whole-wheat flour
¼ teaspoon baking powder
1 teaspoon baking soda
2 teaspoons ground cinnamon
½ teaspoon grated nutmeg
1 cup chopped pecans

1. Preheat oven to 350°F (175°C). Generously grease and flour two
    9 x 5-inch loaf pans.
2. In a large bowl, beat eggs until light and foamy; gradually beat
    in sugar. Continue beating and add vanilla extract and oil. Stir
    in grated zucchini. Sift in dry ingredients and fold in gently. Fold
    in pecans.
3. Divide mixture between prepared pans. Bake 1 to 1¼ hours.
    Cool on wired racks.

Makes 2 loaves.

The zucchini is a small green, light green or yellow squash. Its flower
can be either male or female. The female is the golden blossom on the
end of a baby zucchini. The male flower grows directly on the stem.
Both flowers are edible when firm and fresh. The zucchini is actually
an immature fruit but is treated as a vegetable, and it is usually offered
as a savory dish or as an accompaniment. Easy to grow, it is a favorite
here in New Mexico.

MAIN DISHES

Following is a collection of specially-selected recipes—some old favorites chosen to give you the true taste of traditional New Mexico cuisine as well as modern, more eclectic recipes, reflecting the newer trends in Southwestern cooking. Because the recipes vary in ingredients and complexity, you should have little trouble selecting one for any occasion and any cook.

Whenever we have guests at home, they always ask if I'm going to make Chicken Fajitas. This recipe can establish your reputation as a great New Mexico cook. Because your guests assemble their own fajitas from side dishes, they will suit their own tastes and give you credit—a definite win-win situation. The word "fajitas" in Spanish means "little belts," which the strips of chicken or beef seem to resemble.

Chile Rellenos present large green chiles as a vegetable entree. Stuffed with cheese, batter coated and quickly deep fried, the chile pepper is presented in its glory. No taste can compare to that of this dish when made with fresh green New Mexico chiles. You'll enjoy this great treat even if you use frozen or canned chiles.

Although I've no proof, I think Chicken-Fried Steak was invented in New Mexico. Perhaps it is the quality of beef we raise here or my years of experience serving it—but whatever the case, we do it right. Follow my formula for a melt-in-your-mouth dish that is guaranteed to impress any guest.

I have also included several recipes that show you how to utilize left-over chili. I think you will find my vegetarian chili especially versatile. It freezes well and is quite useful, as you will see.

Baked Chili Tamales

Not traditional tamales but you will be pleased with the results. An excellent way to use your leftover chili.

⅓ cup shortening
1 teaspoon salt
½ teaspoon baking powder
2 cups masa harina or cornmeal
1½ cups chicken broth
2 cups Sweet Chili (See page 136) or Vegetarian Chili (See page 137)
1 cup longhorn cheese, shredded

1. Preheat oven to 350°F (175°C). Grease a 13 x 9-inch pan.
2. In a small bowl, beat shortening until light and creamy.
3. In a medium bowl, combine salt, baking powder, and masa harina or cornmeal. Beat in shortening, a small amount at a time. Beat in chicken broth to make a soft, light dough.
4. Spread half of the dough in bottom of greased pan. Spoon chili over dough.
5. Spread remaining dough over the chili.
6. Bake in preheated oven for about 45 minutes.
7. Cut into 8 tamales. Sprinkle with shredded cheese and serve immediately.

Makes 8 tamales.

The *tamale* is a traditional New Mexican food consisting of steam-cooked corn flour dough (masa harina) with or without filling. Tamales can be filled with meats, cheeses and sliced chiles, or any combination according to one's tastes. Generally wrapped in corn husks, tamales were originally developed as a portable food ration in ancient times. A favorite dish, tamales are considered by many to be the New Mexican equivalent of sandwiches.

Baked Yam Flautas with Piñon Nuts & Sesame Seeds

I think that every cook likes to show off and here's a dish to help when you want to impress someone special. The yams make an especially flavorful filling. This versatile dish can be served as a main dish, fancy side dish, perhaps even a dessert.

2 pounds yams or winter squash (acorn, banana or hubbard), halved
    and seeded
6 tablespoons butter
1 teaspoon sugar
6 softened flour tortillas
½ cup piñon nuts
2 tablespoons sesame seeds
1 tablespoon confectioners' sugar
1 cup dairy sour cream

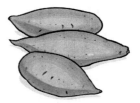

1. Heat oven to 375°F (190°C). Place yams or squash pieces in oven and bake 60 to 90 minutes, until soft in the center.
2. Remove pulp from yams or squash and place in bowl; add 2 tablespoons of butter and 1 teaspoon of sugar. Stir with fork.
3. Place about ⅓ cup yam or squash filling in center of each tortilla.
4. Roll up softened tortilla, folding ends in and sealing in the filling. Secure with wooden pick. Set aside.
5. In an ungreased skillet, combine piñon nuts and sesame seeds. Stirring over medium heat, toast 2 to 3 minutes, until browned.
6. In a large frying pan, over medium heat, melt 2 tablespoons of butter until foaming. Add half of the flautas. Turning as necessary, fry until brown and crisp, about 2 minutes.
7. Remove to warm platter. Add remaining butter to skillet and continue frying remaining flautas until all are cooked.
8. Sir confectioner's sugar into dairy sour cream. Top each flautas with sweetened dairy sour cream. Sprinkle roasted piñon nuts and sesame seeds on top. Serve warm and crunchy.

Makes 6 servings

Bean Chimichangas

Some folks like to microwave this dish after step #4 and then serve with green or red chile sauce. There are many different fillings used in this traditional dish but I like this one.

6 large flour tortillas
¾ cup Refried Pinto Beans (See page 28)
2 4-ounce cans New Mexico green chiles, drained and chopped
    OR 6 to 10 fresh or frozen green chiles, roasted, peeled, seeded, de-veined and chopped
¾ cup grated longhorn cheese
1 cup dairy sour cream
¾ cup Guacamole (See page 20)
salsa of choice, to taste
1 cup shredded lettuce
1 cup peeled and chopped tomatoes

1. Warm tortillas (See page 55).
2. In a small saucepan, heat refried pinto beans and chiles.
3. In the center of each tortilla, spread refried beans and chiles; sprinkle with cheese.
4. Fold edges of tortilla in center, overlapping.
5. Place seam side down on a warmed serving plate; top with sour cream.
6. Spoon guacamole on top of sour cream. Spoon salsa over ends.
Garnish with lettuce and tomatoes.

Makes 6 servings.

Folks in Arizona call this dish a Burro or a Sonora Taco. Chimichangas there are deep-fried. This is another example of the difference between New Mexico cuisine and Southwest or Tex-Mex cuisine.

Burritos with Bacon & Avocado

In recent years, the burrito has replaced the taco as the most requested menu item here in New Mexico. Burritos can be made with endless varieties of fillings and are easy to prepare. There are even fast food franchises built on this popular offering. Here is one variety.

3 eggs
1½ tablespoons milk
2 tablespoons vegetable oil
1½ cup shredded Cheddar cheese
1 cup chopped green onions
¾ pound sliced bacon, cooked and crumbled
6 flour tortillas
1 ripe avocado, thinly sliced
salt and pepper to taste
salsa, ranch dressing or sour cream

1. Beat eggs and mix in milk.
2. In a skillet, add vegetable oil and cook egg mixture until firm, turning as needed. Salt and pepper to taste.
3. Warm tortillas (See page 55).
4. Place equal portions of eggs, bacon, green onions and cheese in center of each tortilla.
5. Wrap each tortilla, folding the ends and sides over the filling. If desired, filled burritos may be warmed in microwave just before serving.
6. Top with avocado slices, salsa, ranch dressing or sour cream.

Serves 6

Carne Asada Tacos—Taqueria Style

Taquería (sometimes anglicized to *taquiria*) is a Spanish word meaning taco shop. Although taquerías were originally street vendors in Mexico, today in some localities the term is used to refer to restaurants specializing in burritos and other dishes as well as tacos. This variation uses the lesser known flap steak and is made with soft corn tortillas rather than flour tortillas.

¼ cup olive oil
6 garlic cloves
2 tablespoons lime juice
½ teaspoon dried-leaf rosemary
½ teaspoon ground red New Mexico chile
¼ teaspoon powdered Mexican oregano
¼ teaspoon ground cumin
2 pounds flap steak
1 tablespoon vegetable oil
3 medium white onions, cut into ½-inch slices
6 warmed corn tortillas
red or green sauce or salsa of choice (See Sauces or Salsa pages 139–149), Guacamole (See page 20)

1. In a blender or food processor, puree ½ of the olive oil, garlic, lime juice, rosemary, chile, oregano and cumin.
2. Rub garlic-herb paste on both sides of steaks.
3. Broil steaks 4 inches from heat source for 6 to 8 minutes per side.
4. In a small skillet, heat vegetable oil and cook onions until soft. OR grill steaks and onion slices over medium heat until steak is medium rare, 12 to 15 minutes. Turn once. Onions should become tender in 15 minutes.
5. Thinly slice steaks across grain. Serve wrapped in warm tortillas with red or green sauce or salsa and Guacamole.

Makes 4 to 6 servings.

Flap steak is similar to skirt and flank in that it comes from the less tender regions of the animal. Often cheaper than more popular cuts, this little underdog of the beef world has a wonderful meaty flavor and fine texture when prepared carefully. Like skirt or flank steak, flap meat benefits from marinating and being cooked on high, dry heat, whether grilled, broiled, pan-fried or stir-fried. It's vital to cut the meat very thinly across the grain, and it is at its best not much past medium-rare.

Mediterranean and Mexican oregano are two different plants. The taste of Mexican oregano is stronger and less sweet, well-suited for our spicy, hot, cumin-flavored New Mexico cuisine.

Chicken Chilaquiles

A great way to use the new tortilla strips. If they are not yet available in your area markets, you can use stale corn tortillas. Simply place them in between two wet paper towels in the microwave for a few seconds to soften them and cut them into strips. Like enchiladas, chilaquiles can be made in a variety of ways. Here is one easy-to-prepare recipe.

2 cups cubed or shredded cooked chicken
1 10¾-ounce can condensed cream of mushroom soup
1 10¾ ounce can condensed cream of chicken soup
1 cup chicken broth
1 4-ounce can sliced mushrooms
1 4-ounce can New Mexico green chiles, drained and chopped
    OR 3 to 5 fresh or frozen green chiles, roasted, peeled, seeded,
    de-veined and chopped
1 cup sour cream
1 cup white onions, chopped
1 8-ounce bag of tortilla strips
1 cup grated Monterey Jack cheese

1. Preheat oven to 350°F (175°C).
2. Mix together chicken, soups, broth, mushrooms, chiles and sour cream.
3. Layer bottom of a greased 9 x 12-inch casserole with half of the tortilla strips.
4. Add half of chicken soup mixture, onions and cheese.
5. Repeat layer of strips, then add remaining mixture, remaining onion and balance of cheese on top.
Bake for 30 minutes.

Serves 6.

The Rio Grande River runs from Colorado to the Texas-Mexico border and through the center of New Mexico. It rushes down narrow gorges in the north then lazily wanders out onto the fertile valleys of the south. The Rio Grande is our primary source of water; however, six other rivers in the Land of Enchantment are also important to our economy: the Pecos, Canadian, Chama, San Juan, Brazos and Gila.

Chicken Fajitas

This is my personal favorite New Mexico dish. When I go into a new restaurant, this is the dish I order to check out the cook. If he or she can do this one right, chances are the rest of the menu will be worth trying. When I want to show off, this is the meal I always prepare.

2 pounds skinless, boned chicken breasts
1 teaspoon peeled, grated fresh ginger
2 garlic cloves, minced
1 cup light soy sauce
¼ cup fresh orange juice
¼ cup fresh lime juice
2 tablespoons honey
2 tablespoons extra virgin olive oil or vegetable oil
2 large white onions, sliced
1½ green bell peppers, seeded, de-veined and thinly sliced
1½ red bell peppers, seeded, de-veined and thinly sliced
salt to taste

12 flour tortillas

Side dishes

½ cup Refried Pinto Beans (See page 28)
1 cup Guacamole (See page 20)
4 cups shredded lettuce
1 cup grated Monterey Jack cheese
1 cup dairy sour cream

salsa or chili sauce of choice

Note: Refried beans, guacamole, shredded lettuce, grated cheese, salsa or sauce and sour cream should be prepared ahead of cooking the chicken and be served as side dishes. Tortillas should be served hot in covered container.

1. Place a piece of waxed paper or plastic wrap on a cutting board. Place each chicken breast on top and cover with another piece of waxed paper or plastic wrap. With a mallet, flatten chicken breasts to ⅛-one-eighth-inch thick. Set aside.
2. In a large bowl, combine ginger, garlic, soy sauce, orange juice, lime juice and honey. Add chicken; refrigerate in marinade 3 to 6 hours. You may also marinate in a plastic bag if you prefer.
3. About 10 minutes before cooking, drain chicken and pat dry. Grill or broil chicken until no longer pink, but still moist, about 1½ minutes per side. Remove from grill or broiler, slice across the grain into 1¼-inch strips; cover and set aside.
4. In a deep non-stick skillet, heat oil until very hot. Add onions and bell peppers; sauté.
   Add chicken strips and toss together. Season with salt to taste. Serve immediately on very hot plate, preferably a metal sizzle platter.
5. To assemble fajitas, place a portion of hot chicken mixture in center of tortilla and top with side dishes. Fold tortilla, closing one end. Eat as hand food (but you may need a fork at the end!). If you are serving guests, place all the side dishes on the table and have them assemble their own fajitas according to their own tastes.

Makes 6 servings.

New Mexico is commonly thought to have Spanish as an official language alongside English, due to the widespread usage of Spanish in our state. Although the original state constitution of 1912 did provide for a temporarily bilingual government, to date New Mexico has adopted no official language. Nevertheless, the state government publishes election ballots and a drivers' manual in both languages.

The constitution provided that, for the following twenty years after 1912, all laws passed by the legislature had to be published in both Spanish and English, and thereafter as the legislature should provide. After 1967, notices of statewide and county elections were required to be printed in English and "may be printed in Spanish."

Additionally, many legal notices today are required to be published in both English and Spanish. In 1995, New Mexico adopted a State Bilingual Song titled "New Mexico—Mi Lindo Nuevo Mexico" by Pablo Mares. The original State Song was written in English as "Oh Fair New Mexico" by Elizabeth Garrett, daughter of former Lincoln County Sheriff Pat Garrett, the man who shot Billy the Kid.

Chicken-Friend Steak with Cream Gravy

This is an old ranch recipe from my youth. My Aunt Tiny, a great cook, had real buttermilk to marinate her steaks. Today buttermilk is made by adding special bacteria to nonfat or lowfat milk. This works for a marinade, just not quite as well as the old real buttermilk did.

4 cups buttermilk
6 7-ounce round steaks
salt and pepper to taste
5 eggs
1 12-ounce can evaporated milk
½ cup vegetable oil
3 tablespoons all-purpose flour
2 cups water

1. Pound steak with meat with tenderizing mallet (or have your butcher tenderize them). Pour buttermilk into a shallow dish; add steaks and marinate at least 2 hours. Remove from dish and discard buttermilk.
2. Sprinkle steak with salt and pepper; set aside. Beat eggs and ½ cup evaporated milk together in a bowl. Heat oil in a deep-sided skillet to 350°F (175°C).
3. Dredge steaks with flour; dip in egg batter. Flour again lightly; shake off excess flour.
4. Add steaks to skillet one at a time; do not allow the temperature to drop. Fry 4 minutes, or until golden brown; turn to fry other side until golden brown. Remove from skillet; drain on paper towels. Keep warm in warm oven (150°F [65°C]).
5. Prepare gravy by pouring all but 4 teaspoons oil from skillet and reduce heat to low. Add 2 tablespoons flour to skillet. Stirring constantly, cook until flour is brown.
6. Add rest of evaporated milk, whisking mixture until smooth, scraping the bottom of the skillet to pick up remaining material.
7. Add water gradually, stirring constantly, until all is added and gravy is smooth and thickened. Add salt and pepper to taste. Serve separately.

Makes 6 servings.

Chicken Ranchero

For the family or company, this is an excellent way to serve chicken. I especially like poaching the breasts before baking them.

4 chicken breasts
3 large tomatoes, finely chopped
1 4-ounce can New Mexico green chiles, drained and chopped
    OR 3 to 5 fresh or frozen green chiles, roasted, peeled, seeded, de-veined and chopped
1 white onion, finely chopped
1 cup chicken broth
salt to taste
1 jalapeño, seeded and finely chopped
2 tablespoons all-purpose flour
2 tablespoons red chili powder
3 tablespoons vegetable oil
2½ cups water
½ teaspoon salt
1 cup grated Monterey Jack cheese

1. Poach chicken breasts in boiling, salted water for 10 minutes.
2. Preheat oven to 450°F (225°C).
3. In a saucepan, mix together tomatoes, green chiles, onion and chicken broth. Bring to a boil. Cover and simmer ½ hour or until vegetables are soft. Add salt to taste and jalapeño pepper.
4. In another pan, blend flour, chili powder and oil. Add water and salt and bring to a boil. Lower heat and simmer gently for 5 minutes, stirring occasionally.
5. Pour sauce into 9-inch square baking dish and place chicken breasts on top of sauce.
6. Pour green chile and tomato sauce over the chicken breasts and sprinkle generously with grated cheese.
7. Bake uncovered 15 to 20 minutes, until chicken is tender and cheese is melted.

Makes 4 servings.

If your dishwasher has stains in it, try filling your soap dispenser with Powdered Gatoraid© and run it through a complete cycle.

Chile Rellenos

Each year I wait for the new crop of green chiles to become available, and the first dish I prepare is Chile Rellenos. I know of no better way to enjoy fresh chiles.

8 poblano or New Mexico green chiles, roasted and peeled.
½ pound longhorn, Cheddar or Monterey Jack cheese
3 cups oil for frying
1 cup all-purpose flour
½ teaspoon salt
½ teaspoon sugar
pinch of baking soda
1 egg
½ teaspoon oil
1 cup ice water
red or green sauce or salsa of choice (See Sauces or Salsa pages 139-149)

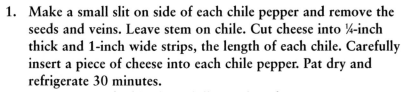

1. Make a small slit on side of each chile pepper and remove the seeds and veins. Leave stem on chile. Cut cheese into ¼-inch thick and 1-inch wide strips, the length of each chile. Carefully insert a piece of cheese into each chile pepper. Pat dry and refrigerate 30 minutes.
2. Heat 3 cups of oil in deep skillet or deep fryer to 375°F (190°C).
3. In a medium bowl, combine flour, salt, sugar and baking soda. In a cup, beat egg, oil and cold water together with fork. Combine with flour mixture. Do not over mix. Use at once.
4. Dip chiles one at a time into batter. Allow excess batter to drip off. Slide each coated chile gently into hot oil. Fry until golden brown on both sides. Drain on paper towels.

Serve immediately with red or green sauce or salsa on top.

Makes 4 servings.

Zuni Pueblo, the largest of New Mexico's pueblos, is located 38 miles south of Gallup on NM 32. Zuni artisans are best known for their magnificently detailed jewelry and pottery as well as their fetish carvings.

Chile Rellenos Sausage Casserole

During my many trips to this Land of Enchantment before we moved here, I used to stop at a little roadside restaurant in Taos. This was the breakfast specialty of the house.

3 eggs
1 cup evaporated milk
1 tablespoon all-purpose flour
½ pound pork sausage
1 4-ounce can New Mexico green chiles, drained
    OR 3 to 5 fresh or frozen green chiles, roasted, peeled, seeded and de-veined
1 cup grated longhorn or Monterey Jack cheese
¼ teaspoon paprika

1. Preheat oven to 350°F (175°C). Generously grease an 8-inch casserole.
2. In a bowl, beat eggs, milk and flour.
3. In skillet, brown sausage and pour off grease.
4. Drain chiles, split and layer in bottom of prepared casserole.
5. Top with sausage and cheese. Pour egg mixture over top. Sprinkle with paprika.
6. Bake in preheated oven for about 30 minutes, until top is firm and brown.

Makes 4 servings.

In 1821, under the treaty of Cordova, Mexico won independence from Spain. With independence came dominion over a vast territory that had been Spanish land. This Mexican period lasted for 25 years until Brigadier-General Stephen Watts Kearny hoisted the American flag over the Palace of Governors in Santa Fe on August 18, 1846. The Mexican War (1846-1848) and the discovery of gold in California caused a heavy increase in traffic along the Old Santa Fe Trail. Fort Union was established as a base for military troops and a rest stop for weary travelers.

Chile Soufflé

If you have company and want to show off, here's a great recipe that's easy to prepare and a nice way to start the day. I got it from a cowboy cook at the chuckwagon cook-off in Clovis, New Mexico. He cooked his in a Dutch oven over a bed of hot coals. I do mine in the oven. Give it try.

3 teaspoons butter
3 tablespoons all purpose flour
1 cup milk
3 egg yolks
½ cup cottage cheese
½ cup chopped drained tomato pulp
2 tablespoons chopped green onions
3 New Mexico green chiles, roasted, peeled, seeded and chopped
    or 1 4-ounce can chopped New Mexico green chiles, drained
3 egg whites
salt and black pepper to taste

1. Preheat oven to 350°F (175°C).
2. Melt butter in a saucepan and stir in flour.
3. Using a whisk, blend in milk. Cook over medium heat until thick.
4. Remove from heat and whisk in egg yolks, one at a time. Fold in cottage cheese, tomato pulp, onions and chiles. Salt and pepper to taste
5. In a separate bowl, beat egg whites until they form stiff peaks. Thoroughly fold about half the egg whites into yolk mixture. Add the remaining egg whites by folding in quickly, leaving some streaks of white.
6. Pour into a prepared one-quart soufflé dish.
7. Bake 30–35 minutes, until deep golden brown.

Serves 4.

Chili Tostados

Tostados are fun. Each person can assemble them to suit his or her individual taste. Tostados are good way to serve leftover chili and have a quick, easy meal.

5 tablespoons peanut or vegetable oil
8 corn tortillas
2 cups Refried Beans (See page 28)
1½ cups Cowpoke Chili (See page 128) or Gringo Chili (See page 129), heated
1 cup iceberg lettuce, shredded
1 cup Guacamole (See page 20)
1 tomato, chopped
½ cup Monterey Jack cheese, shredded

1. To prepare tortillas, first heat oil in a small skillet on medium high heat, until bubbles form immediately when you insert the edge of a tortilla. Using tongs, place each tortilla in hot oil and let cook until golden brown on both sides, about 30 seconds per side. You can use spatula to flatten down tortilla as it cooks. Remove tortilla with tongs and allow excess oil to drip off.
2. Spread ¼ cup refried beans evenly on top of each tortilla and top with 2 tablespoons of heated chili of choice.
3. Spread shredded lettuce on top of each tostado and spoon on guacamole. Sprinkle with tomatoes and cheese.

Makes 4 servings of 2 tostados each.

The Taos Society of Artists was founded in 1912 and was composed of some of America's finest artists. Today the paintings by its members bring some of the American art's highest prices. Members included such greats as Ernest Blumenschein, Henry Sharp, Bert Phillips, Oscar Berninghaus, Herbert Dunton and E. Irving Couse. Artists in the Taos Society distinguished themselves as nationally recognized realists and romantic painters of the West through exhibitions that circulated throughout the country between 1915 and 1927. At the same time, some 100 miles to the south of Taos, the Santa Fe Art Colony began to form, as younger, more experimental artists flocked there to search for scenic and inexpensive places to work.

Cowboy Casserole

Here's a stick-to-your-ribs brunch dish or main menu offering that I always prepare when we have guests staying with us. It takes about 5 minutes to prepare and a little less than an hour to bake. You can adjust the heat level easily by the green chile type you use.

3 tablespoons butter
1 small white onion, chopped
4 cups store-bought, shredded hash browns
1 pound bulk pork sausage, mild, hot or sage
½ cup whole milk
8 large eggs
1 teaspoon salt
¼ teaspoon black pepper
¼ teaspoon fresh ground nutmeg
2 tablespoons Dijon mustard
2 4-ounce cans New Mexico green chiles, drained and chopped
   OR 6 to 10 fresh or frozen green chiles, roasted, peeled, seeded, de-veined and chopped
8 cups any kind of day old bread, cubed with crusts removed
2 cups (½ pound) grated Cheddar cheese
2 cups (½ pound) freshly grated Parmesan cheese
your favorite Red or Green Chile Sauce (Or see page 139)

1. Preheat oven to 350°F (175°C).
2. Spray a deep 13 x 16-inch casserole dish with vegetable oil
3. In a large frying pan, melt butter. Add onion and sauté over medium-low heat until soft, about 5 minutes. Add hash browns and break apart. Sauté until soft, about 5 minutes.
4. In a second frying pan. Sauté sausage, breaking apart large clumps. When it is cooked remove from pan.
5. In a large mixing bowl, combine milk, eggs, salt, pepper, nutmeg and mustard. Whip briskly.
6. To assemble, spread the onions and hash browns evenly on the bottom of sprayed dish. Place bread cubes evenly on top of hash

browns. On top of bread cubes spread sausage and green chiles evenly as a third layer. Pour whipped egg and milk over these layers. Use Parmesan cheese as next layer and then Cheddar cheese as sixth layer. Bake the casserole uncovered for 45 to 50 minutes, until puffed and golden brown.
Serve with red or green chile sauce of choice.

Makes 6 to 8 servings.

I usually reserve a few teaspoons of Cheddar cheese and add it as a fresh topping about 10 minutes before the casserole is ready to come out of the oven.

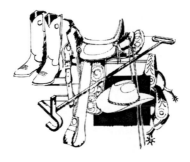

Enchiladas Verdes

This is an old Mexican version of enchiladas, now common here in New Mexico. The rich, full-flavored dish uses rolled tortillas.

2 whole chicken breasts
1 cup chicken broth
2 3-ounce packages cream cheese
2 cups heavy cream
¾ cup finely chopped white onions
4 green bell peppers, seeded, de-veined and coarsely chopped.
1 10-ounce can tomatillos, drained
2 4-ounce cans New Mexico green chiles, drained and chopped
  OR 6 to 10 fresh or frozen green chiles, roasted, peeled, seeded, de-veined and chopped
2 teaspoons ground coriander
1 egg
1½ teaspoons salt
freshly ground black pepper to taste
3 tablespoons vegetable oil
12 corn tortillas
½ cup grated Parmesan cheese

1. Cook chicken in broth for about 20 minutes or until tender. Shred meat set aside.
2. In a large mixing bowl, beat cream cheese until smooth. Beat in ½ cup of cream, small amounts at a time. Stir in onions and shredded chicken. Mix well and set aside.
3. Place bell peppers in a blender or food processor. Add tomatillos, green chiles, coriander and ¼ cup reserved chicken broth. Blend at high speed until contents are reduced to a smooth puree.
4. Pour in remaining cream, egg, salt, ground black pepper and blend for 10 seconds.
5. Place mixture in a large bowl. Preheat oven to 350°F (174°C).

6. In a heavy 8 to 10-inch skillet, heat oil until very hot. Using tongs dip each tortilla in chile mixture and carefully slide into skillet. Spattering may occur. Fry for a minute or so both sides.

7. Transfer tortilla from skillet to a plate; place ¼ cup chicken filling in center. Fold one side of the tortilla over the filling and roll into a thick cylinder. Place seam side down in a 13 X 9-inch baking dish. Fry and fill the remaining tortillas in the same manner replenishing oil as necessary.

8. Pour remaining sauce over filled tortillas in dish. Sprinkle with Parmesan cheese. Bake in preheated oven for about 20 minute until cheese melts and enchiladas brown on top. Serve at once.

Makes 6 servings.

nchiladas with Green Chiles

This is an old traditional New Mexico enchilada recipe. This style of layered enchilada is typical here. I prefer this presentation.

1 4-ounce can New Mexico green chiles, drained and cut into
    thumb-sized pieces
    OR 3 to 5 fresh or frozen green chiles, roasted, peeled, seeded,
    de-veined and cut into thumb-sized pieces
1 tablespoon oil
1½ pound lean ground beef
salt and fresh ground black pepper to taste
water to cover (see below)
oil for frying
12 corn tortillas
½ cup Enchilada Sauce (See page 145)
2 cups grated Cheddar or Monterey Jack cheese
1 small white onion chopped

1. In a skillet, heat 1 tablespoon oil. Add meat and brown; season with salt and pepper.
2. Stir in chiles and cover with water. Cook 20 minutes. Preheat oven to 250°F (120°C).
3. In a skillet, heat small amount of oil. Fry each tortilla until firm. Using tongs, remove from oil, shaking off excess. Dip in enchilada sauce, covering entire surface; remove and place on an ovenproof plate or shallow casserole and top with a spoonful of meat/chile mixture, cheese and onions. Repeat until tortillas are stacked 3 high on each plate. Spoon remaining chile-meat mixture over each stack; sprinkle with cheese, bake in preheated oven for 20 minutes and serve.

Makes 4 servings.

There are many styles of enchiladas. In other Southwestern states, folks sometimes start with uncooked corn tortillas that are placed in a casserole dish and alternately layered with cooked parceled chicken breast, chiles and grated Cheddar or Monterey Jack cheese. This is then covered with chicken soup, topped with grated cheese and baked until done. See my recipe for this style, Mexican Casserole (See Page 98).

Green Chile Pork Stew

This basic New Mexico stew has as many variations as there are cooks. I especially like this version.

2 pounds lean pork, cubed
2 tablespoons vegetable oil
1 large white onion, chopped
2 garlic cloves, minced
2 4-ounce cans New Mexico green chiles, drained and chopped
OR 6 to 10 fresh or frozen green chiles, roasted, peeled, seeded, de-veined and chopped
1 large potato, peeled and diced
2 tomatoes, peeled, seeded and chopped
3 to 4 cups water
½ teaspoon dried leaf Mexican oregano

1. In a large skillet, brown the pork in the oil. Remove pork and place in a kettle or stockpot.
2. Put onions in skillet, adding more oil if necessary, and sauté until they are soft.
3. Add garlic and cook for an few additional minutes. Remove onions and garlic and add to stockpot. Pour a little of the water into the skillet, bring to a boil and deglaze.
4. Pour liquid from skillet over the pork. Add all remaining ingredients, cover and simmer for 1 to 2 hours, or until meat is very tender and starting to fall apart.

Serves 4 to 6.

Founded in 1706, Albuquerque is the largest city in New Mexico. Situated in the center of the state, it straddles the Rio Grande River. Beginning during the Mexican war, Albuquerque was a very important U.S. military post from 1846 to 1870. The city grew as a farming hub and health center, and it was incorporated in 1891. Starting in the 1950s its population began to greatly expand due to federal spending on nuclear research and an influx of technology-based industry. In the 1970s the city underwent an extensive urban renewal program, culminating in the 80s with the completed expansion of the convention center and airport. In 2006 Albuquerque celebrated its tricentennial.

Indian Tacos

Here is a great way to use the Navajo Fry Bread (See page 66). This dish is often featured at Indian powwows and other festivals.

1 pound lean ground meat (beef, lamb, venison or pork.)
1 cup diced white onion
1 clove garlic, minced
4 Navajo Fry Breads
½ head of lettuce, shredded
3 tomatoes, seeded and diced
2 cups shredded cheese of choice
1 4-ounce can New Mexico green chiles, drained and chopped
      or 3 to 5 fresh or frozen green chiles, roasted, peeled, seeded,
      de-veined and chopped
dairy sour cream

1. In a large-size frying pan, over medium heat, brown meat, onions and garlic. Remove from heat.
2. Place individual fry breads cupped side up on plates. Layer meat, lettuce, tomatoes, cheese and green chiles on top of each. Serve open faced, topped with sour cream.

Makes 4 servings.

In early times the typical diet of the Navajos was composed of beans, corn, squash and wild game. They also raised sheep for mutton and wool. Wild foods were important, including wild celery and onion, Navajo spinach (beeweed and pigweed), wolfberries, wax current berries, sumac berries, juniper berries, yucca banana fruits and Navajo tea (Thelesperma). Protein came from mutton, venison, piñon nuts, squash seeds, tumble mustard seeds and pinto beans. Also, their goats produced milk for drinking and cheese. Today the Navajo diet has changed to more typically American, with obesity and alcoholism as serious problems.

Meatballs in Chile Sauce

Meatballs in Chile Sauce can be served over pasta or rice. Because it freezes well, double the recipe and freeze half. When guests arrive you will have a quick meal ready in no time using the frozen half.

3 corn tortillas, cut into pieces
½ cup milk
½ pound ground beef
½ pound ground pork
½ pound smoked ham, chopped
¼ cup white onion, chopped
1 garlic clove, finely chopped
1 teaspoon ground cumin
1 teaspoon dried-leaf oregano
salt and black pepper to taste
1 cup Basic Red Sauce (See page 143)
1 cup beef broth
Pasta or rice

1. In a large bowl, place tortilla pieces and milk; let stand for 15 minutes.
2. Mix in remaining ingredients, except for Basic Red Sauce and beef broth.
3. Shape meat mixture into 1-inch balls. In a skillet, brown meatballs on all sides. Remove and set aside.
4. In a 10-inch skillet, heat Basic Red Sauce and beef broth. Bring to a boil; reduce heat, add meat balls.
5. Cover and simmer until done. Serve over cooked pasta or rice.

Makes 6 servings.

Most food colorings are artificial and have little or no nutritional value but are used to make food appear more appealing to the consumer (for example maraschino cherries), but some food colorings are natural. For example, a large quantity of chiles grown in and around where I live in Roswell, New Mexico, are actually flavorless and used for food coloring.

Mexican Casserole

Simple and quick, try using fresh corn from the cob and fresh green New Mexico chiles when in season. For different flavors, change and combine cheeses.

1 pound ground beef
½ white onion, chopped
salt and black pepper to taste
1 8-ounce can kernel corn, drained
1 4-ounce can New Mexico green chiles, drained and diced
    OR 3 to 5 fresh or frozen green chiles, roasted, peeled, seeded, de-veined and diced
1 10½-ounce can cream of mushroom soup
8 corn tortillas
8 ounces shredded Cheddar cheese

1. Preheat oven to 350°F (175°C). Lightly grease a 2-quart casserole.
2. In a 10-inch skillet, brown meat and onion. Add salt and pepper to taste.
3. Add corn, green chiles and mushroom soup; mix well.
4. In a greased casserole, alternate layers of tortillas, meat mixture and cheese. The top layer should be cheese.
5. Bake in preheated oven for about 20 minutes, until brown and bubbly.

Makes 8 servings.

Picadillo over Rice

Picadillo is an excellent filling for tacos, tamales and chile rellenos; any recipe calling for a meat filling can use this. Try sausage instead of pork for an additional taste treat.

½ pound ground beef
½ pound ground pork
1 cup chopped white onion
2 garlic cloves, minced
1 16-ounce can tomatoes, drained and chopped
1 tablespoon vinegar
½ teaspoon ground cinnamon
1 pinch ground cloves
¼ teaspoon ground cumin
1 teaspoon salt
1 bay leaf
⅛ teaspoon Tabasco sauce
1 teaspoon ground red chile
½ cup seedless raisins
½ cup green olives, chopped
½ cup blanched slivered almonds
2 cups cooked rice

1. In a 10-inch skillet, stir meats over high heat. When meat begins to cook add onion and garlic.
2. After meat browns, pour off excess fat; add remaining ingredients except raisins, olives and almonds.
3. Reduce heat to simmer, cover and cook 30 minutes
4. Add water if necessary. Picadillo should be moist, but not soupy.
5. Add raisins, olives and almonds. Continue cooking for 10 minutes.
Serve over cooked rice.

Makes 4 servings.

Pork Fajitas

Here is a chance for you to try Ancho Mole Sauce (See page 141) You will note that I use unsweetened chocolate. If you can find Mexican chocolate, use it in making your Mole Sauce for a richer taste.

4 pounds pork tenderloin
¼ cup Ancho Mole Sauce
½ cup freshly squeezed lemon juice
4 garlic cloves, crushed
¼ teaspoon black peppercorns
1 tablespoon water
1½ teaspoons salt or to taste
8 corn tortillas
1 lemon cut in wedges
1 cup iceberg lettuce, shredded
1 tomato, seeded and diced
½ cup white onion, chopped
Guacamole (See page 20)
Dairy sour cream

1. Trim tenderloin of excess fat and all silver skin. In a large bowl, mix mole sauce, lemon juice, garlic, peppercorns, water and salt. Place mixture and tenderloin in plastic bag to marinade and refrigerate overnight.
2. The following day, salt and grill tenderloin until done, about 15 minutes, turning once or twice during grilling. For a special flavor, use mesquite wood chips in the fire. For best results allow meat to rest for 10 minutes before slicing.
3. Before serving, wrap tortillas in foil and heat in 275°F (135°C) oven. To serve, place strips of tenderloin down center of warmed tortillas and top with remaining garnishes to taste.

Makes 4 servings.

Pork tenderloin is one of the leanest meats available, and according to the National Pork Producers' comparison chart, it's nearly as low in saturated fat as chicken breast. The tenderloin is part of the loin, and you can usually find it sold separately in packages of two. There's very little fat on a tenderloin, so a small amount can go a long ways, particularly in stir-fry dishes.

Santa Fe Steak

Sometimes referred to as Round Steak Rolls, this recipe rolls the steak and adds onion soup for a nice change of pace. Here in New Mexico we have some of the finest cattle ranches in the United states and a great meat selection.

1½ pound round steak, cut ¼-inch thick by butcher
salt and black pepper, to taste
1 4-ounce can New Mexico green chiles, drained and cut in halves
    OR 3 to 5 fresh or frozen green chiles, roasted, peeled, seeded,
    de-veined and cut in halves
½ cup butter or oil
1 garlic clove, minced
2 cups fresh bread crumbs
3 tablespoons chopped parsley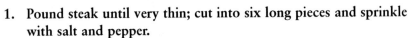
2 hard-cooked eggs, chopped
¼ cup Parmesan cheese
1 10½-ounce can condensed onion soup
½ cup chopped fresh mushrooms
1 cup dry red wine
cooked noodles or rice

1. Pound steak until very thin; cut into six long pieces and sprinkle with salt and pepper.
2. Place halved chiles over strips of meat.
3. In a medium-sized skillet, heat ¼ cup butter; sauté garlic until golden brown. Add bread crumbs to skillet and sauté until golden brow.
4. Remove from heat. Stir in parsley, hard cooked eggs and Parmesan cheese.
5. Spoon mixture into each piece of meat. Roll up and fasten with toothpicks.
6. In a large skillet, heat remaining ¼ cup butter and brown meat roll-ups on all sides.
7. Add onion soup, mushrooms and wine. Cover and simmer 1 hour, or until meat is tender.
Serve with noodles or rice.

Makes 6 servings.

Southwest Riblets

Looking for a feisty-flavored dish? You just found it! Here are pork ribs as you have never eaten them before. A must for the adventurer in regional cuisines.

½ cup chopped white onion
2 tablespoons vegetable oil
1 tablespoon ground red chiles
6 dried juniper berries, crushed
3 garlic cloves, finely chopped
½ teaspoon salt
½ ounce unsweetened baking chocolate
1 cup water
2 tablespoons cider vinegar
1 6-ounce can tomato paste
2 cups sugar
8 pounds pork back ribs, cut lengthwise across bones

1. In a 2-quart sauce pan, cook and stir onion in oil for 2 minutes. Stir in ground red chiles, juniper berries, garlic and salt. Cover and cook 5 minutes, stirring occasionally. Stir in chocolate until melted.
2. Pour water, vinegar and tomato paste into food processor or blender; blend until smooth. Add onion mixture and sugar; cover and process until well blended.
3. Heat oven to 375°F (190°C)
4. Cut between ribs to separate. Place in a single layer in roasting pan; pour sauce evenly over.
5. Bake uncovered 30 minutes; turn ribs and bake until done, about 30 minutes longer.

Makes 6 servings

Pork back ribs, sometimes called baby backs, are taken form the top of the hog's rib cage between the spine and the spareribs. They have meat between the bones and are shorter and more meaty than spare ribs.

Spicy Lamb Stew

Lamb is available year round here, and it is served often in New Mexico households. If you have not tried it, you should. This simple recipe will acquaint you with its taste.

2 cups lean lamb, cut into cubes
1 large white onion, diced
1 clove garlic, crushed
2 tablespoons olive oil
2 tablespoon all-purpose flour
8 cups beef broth, heated
1 teaspoon ground red chile powder
salt and black pepper to taste
1 4-ounce can New Mexico green chiles, drained and chopped
    or 3 to 5 fresh or frozen green chiles, roasted, peeled, seeded, de-veined and chopped
3 large potatoes, peeled and diced

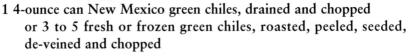

1. In a heavy pan, brown lamb cubes, onion and garlic in olive oil. Stir in flour and cover with heated beef broth.
2. Add chile powder and simmer for 20 minutes. Salt and pepper to taste.
3. Add green chiles and potatoes. Cook over low heat until meat is fork tender, 45 minutes to an hour.

Serves 4.

Stuffed on the Pecos

My wife and I used to feed a herd of teenagers on these. I cooked them outdoors on the barbecue and they were always a hit. Once again, a good way to use your leftover chili.

3 pounds lean ground beef
2 tablespoons onion salt
1½ cups Vegetarian Chili (See page 137) or Jose's Fast Chili (See page 130)
6 tablespoons shredded Cheddar cheese
1 cup black beans or pinto beans
¼ cup black olives, chopped
½ cup green or red bell peppers, seeded and chopped

1. In a medium bowl, mix ground beef and onion salt
2. Divide beef into 12 equal balls; flatten each ball into 5-inch patty.
3. Spoon ¼ cup chili on center of 6 of the patties.
4. Spoon ⅙ of the beans on top of chili.
5. Sprinkle 1 tablespoon of cheese over chili and beans.
6. Place a patty over chili and cheese. Press edges together. Repeat with remaining patties.
7. Heat a large skillet or broiler. Place patties on skillet and cook until well done on both sides, or broil both sides until cooked through, about 12 to 14 minutes. For grilling, wrap patties in foil.

Garnish with black olives and bell peppers

Makes 6 servings.

We some times would increase the selection of items to be stuffed and let each person create his or hers own creation. Use your imagination.

Zucchini, Corn & Pinto Bean Quesadillas

Quesadillas are served like sandwiches here in New Mexico. Use your imagination; the filling can be as varied as your imagination will allow.

1 4-ounce can New Mexico green chiles, drained and chopped
    or 3 to 5 fresh or frozen green chiles, roasted, peeled, seeded, de-veined and chopped
1 cup zucchini, grated and drained on paper towels
1 cup defrosted frozen corn, drained on paper towels.
1 white onion, chopped
1 15-ounce can drained and rinsed pinto beans
1 teaspoon ground chili powder
¼ teaspoon fresh ground black pepper
¾ pound Monterey jack cheese, grated
12 large flour tortillas
2 tablespoons cooking oil

1. In a large bowl, combine green chiles, zucchini, corn, onion, beans, chili powder, black pepper and cheese. Toss to mix.
2. On six tortillas, place approximately on sixth of the mixture in center. Moisten tortilla edges, place additional tortilla on top and press edges to seal. Press to flatten.
3. In a large non-stick frying pan, heat small amount of cooking oil over moderate heat. One at a time, add tortillas to the pan and cook, turning once until the cheese melts, about 1½ minutes per side. Remove from pan and keep warm on a baking sheet in oven. Repeat until all tortillas using the balance of cooking oil.
4. Cut each quesadilla in wedges and serve.

Serves 6.

VEGETABLES & SIDE DISHES

New Mexico's vast irrigated farms grow a large variety of vegetables. The chile pepper reigns supreme here and is considered a vegetable, not just a spice. An impressive number of dishes contain chile peppers used in every possible way. Residents here often send packages of fresh chiles to folks who once lived here and are now deprived of this basic ingredient. I encourage you to use fresh chile peppers whenever possible.

I hope you'll try my squash recipes; they offer new combinations that I think you will find exciting to taste. Squash has always been an important part of New Mexico cooking, and my Peanut Stuffed Acorn Squash makes a delightful brunch entree or the perfect side dish for succulent roast pork or ham.

Of course, I have included a recipe for Pinto Beans that gives you a choice of cooking methods. To guarantee having tender beans, remember to salt beans *after* they have cooked. You can use this versatile ingredient as the basis for a numerous dishes, including soups, salads or main dishes. What a delicious, healthful extender!

Black Beans with Chiles & Tomatoes

This recipe helps you enjoy the deep, very sweet flavor of the black bean. Canned black beans are readily available today.

2 cups cooked or canned black beans with their liquid
2 tablespoons vegetable oil
½ white onion, chopped
1 garlic clove, minced
1 fresh tomato, peeled, seeded and chopped
2 jalapeño peppers, seeded, de-veined and chopped
¼ teaspoon ground cumin
salt and black pepper to taste

1. In a saucepan, heat beans and ½ cup of their liquid to a simmer.
2. In a small skillet, heat oil. Add onion and garlic; cook over low heat until onion is soft.
3. Add remaining ingredients, except beans, and increase heat. Cook over medium heat for 2 minutes, stirring as needed.
4. Place skillet contents in a food processor or blender and puree.
5. Pour pureed mixture into saucepan with beans. Simmer slowly about 5 minutes. Serve at once.

Makes 4 servings.

Black beans have always been around in New Mexico but have been becoming more popular in recent years, partly due to their nutritional value and partly due to their rich flavor. Many Santa Fe restaurants now serve black beans as a side dish rather than the more common pinto beans. Another reason for their increased popularity is that they are a part of the culinary traditions Latin American immigrants are bringing with them. Black bean soups, stews and sauces are very common in Latin American countries, from where they are said to have originated over 7,000 years ago. They have since spread widely around the world, and are commonly used throughout Latin America, the Caribbean and the southern United States (especially Florida and the Southwest).

Calabacitas

This traditional dish is sometimes prepared with fresh chopped tomatoes and served with dairy sour cream. It freezes well for up to four months.

3 tablespoons butter
3 medium-size zucchini, cubed
2 jalapeño chiles, seeded and finely minced
2 cups kernel corn
1 cup milk
½ cup grated Monterey Jack cheese

1. In a large skillet, heat butter and sauté zucchini and onion until tender.
2. Add jalapenos, corn and milk. Simmer mixture 15 to 20 minutes to blend flavors.
3. Add cheese and heat until cheese melts.

Makes 4 servings.

Jalapeños are a pod type of Capsicum. The growing period for a jalapeño plant is 70–80 days. When mature, the plant stands 2½ to 3 feet tall. During the growing period, the jalapeño plant will be picked multiple times. As the growing season comes to an end, the jalapeños start to turn red. The mature red peppers have a richer, warmer flavor but quickly spoil; as a result the fresh market is for green jalapeños. Because of their short shell life, growers often either discard the red jalapeños or use them for the production of chipotles. The chipotle is a smoke-dried red jalapeño.

Calina's Spinach

Here is a great recipe given to me by a friend and great cook, Calina Vasquez. I've never been a great fan of spinach, but I like it prepared in this manner.

2 packages (10 ounces each) frozen, chopped spinach
4 tablespoons unsalted butter
2 tablespoons all-purpose flour
2 tablespoons chopped white onion
½ cup evaporated milk
½ cup spinach cooking water
½ teaspoon black pepper
¾ teaspoon celery salt
¾ teaspoon garlic salt
1 cup Cheddar cheese, grated
1 teaspoon Worcestershire sauce
1 4-ounce can New Mexico green chiles, drained and chopped
    or 3 to 5 fresh or frozen green chiles, roasted, peeled, seeded,
    de-veined and chopped
Buttered breadcrumbs (see below)
salt and black pepper

1. Preheat oven to 350°F (175°C).
2. Cook spinach according to directions on package until done. Drain and reserve ½ cup liquid.
3. In a skillet, sauté onions in ½ of the butter until soft. Blend in flour then add milk and reserved spinach liquid slowly, stirring constantly to avoid lumps. Cook until smooth and thickened.
4. In a small saucepan melt remaining butter and stir in breadcrumbs. Salt and pepper to taste.
5. In a medium-size bowl, mix all ingredients except breadcrumbs together. Pour into a 9-inch-square baking dish and top with crumbs.
6. Bake for 25 minutes.

Makes 6 servings.

Chile & Eggplant

Smaller, immature eggplants are best. If eggplant slices are bitter, salt both sides and set aside for 20 minutes, then rinse and use. This helps get rid of the acid taste.

oil for frying
2 eggs, beaten
¼ cup milk
2 or 3 small eggplants, peeled and sliced crosswise into 1/4-inch pieces.
1 cup toasted breadcrumbs
2 cups canned stewed tomatoes.
2 4-ounce cans New Mexico green chiles, drained and chopped
    OR 6 to 10 fresh or frozen green chiles, roasted, peeled, seeded, de-veined and chopped
1 large white onion, diced
1 pound Longhorn cheese, grated

1. Preheat oven to 350°F (175°C). Heat oil in large skillet.
2. Combine beaten eggs with milk.
3. Dip eggplant slices into egg-milk mixture, then into breadcrumbs. Fry in hot oil until golden brown on both sides.
4. Place half of the eggplant slices in ungreased 13 x 9-inch casserole.
5. Spread half of the stewed tomatoes over the eggplant, then half each of the chiles, diced onion and grated cheese.
6. Place second half of the eggplant slices over mixture. Repeat step 5.
7. Cover and bake in preheated oven 1 hour. Uncover and bake for an additional ½ hour.

Makes 6 servings

Eggplants have many healthful qualities. A source of folic acid and potassium, they can block the formation of free radicals and help lower cholesterol levels. Never eat an eggplant raw as it contains the toxin solanine, which is destroyed by cooking.

Fresh Corn Sauté

This is one of the ways that I have found to use common field corn. Of course, if you have sweet corn available, use it. In New Mexico we grow a lot more field corn than sweet corn.

2 tablespoons olive oil
3 cups corn kernels fresh from the cob
1 jalapeño pepper, seeded and chopped fine
1 red bell pepper, seeded, de-veined and chopped
3 green onions with tops, thinly sliced
⅓ cup milk
¼ cup fresh cilantro, minced
¼ teaspoon freshly ground black pepper
cilantro for garnish

1. Heat olive oil in a large non-stick skillet; sauté corn for 1 minute. Stir in jalapeño and bell peppers. Add green onion, including tops, and sauté about 1 minute.
2. Add milk, cover and simmer about 2 minutes. Uncover and cook, stirring constantly, over high heat until liquid evaporates.
3. Stir in minced fresh cilantro and black pepper.
Garnish with additional fresh cilantro. Serve immediately.

Makes 6 servings.

Rich in tradition and values, the modern community of Española, New Mexico, proudly encompasses many centuries of history. From the time that Spanish explorer Don Juan de Oñate established the first new-world capital there some 400 years ago, Española has been defined by diversity and cultural mobility. Here you will find everything from extraordinary low-rider automobiles to world-class dining and sightseeing. Deep Hispanic family roots coexist easily with contemporary values and practices, giving Española its own unique personality. In July the city commemorates its founding with the Fiesta del Valle de Española. On Christmas Eve, the farolitos and luminarias lining the streets present a distinctively New Mexican scene.

Fried Tomatillos

With hints of lemon, apple and herbs, tomatillos bring a new freshness to this dish. Choose firm fruit with dry, tight-fitting husks.

1¼ pounds fresh tomatillos
¼ cup olive oil or peanut oil
2 onions, quartered, thinly sliced
1 teaspoon salt
⅔ cup whipping cream
12 corn or flour tortillas, warmed
salsa (See page 149 for some ideas, or use your favorite)
1 cup shredded Longhorn cheese

1, Remove outer husks from tomatillos. Rinse and cut in half.
    Cut into thin slices.
2. Heat oil in large skillet until very hot. Add onions and stir to
    coat well. Add tomatillos and salt; cook until tomatillos are soft.
3. Add cream and bring to boil. Immediately remove from heat.
4. To serve, spoon about ½ cup tomatillo mixture on each tortilla.
    Top with salsa and shredded cheese.

Makes 4 servings.

The tomatillo came to us from Mexico in the 1960s. It grows everywhere in the Western Hemisphere and is now common in New Mexico gardens. The plant produces an edible fruit enclosed in a thick husk. The condition of the husk is a good indication of the freshness of the fruit; it should be light brown and fresh looking, not shriveled and dried. Fruit should be yellowish, firm and free of defects.

Indian Squash

Sometimes referred to as Crookneck Stew, I was first introduced to this dish while working in an art foundry just outside Taos New Mexico. It's a wonderful way to prepare the crookneck squash.

2 tablespoons butter
1 small white onion, chopped
2 garlic cloves, minced
2 or 3 yellow crookneck squash, cut into ¼-inch-thick slices
2 fresh tomatoes, peeled and chopped
1 16-ounce can kernel corn, drained
½ teaspoon salt
2 4-ounce cans New Mexico green chiles, drained and chopped
    or 6 to 10 fresh or frozen green chiles, roasted, peeled, seeded,
    de-veined and chopped
¼ teaspoon dried-leaf oregano
½ teaspoon black pepper
1 cup light cream
¼ teaspoon Tabasco sauce
1 3-ounce package cream cheese, cut in cubes

1. In a large heavy skillet, melt butter; add onion and garlic; sauté about 5 minutes over medium heat.
2. Add squash to skillet and continue cooking another 5 minutes, stirring occasionally. Add tomatoes, corn, salt, chile peppers, oregano and black pepper. Reduce heat to low and cook about 20 minutes, until squash is tender. Stir as needed.
3. Stir in light cream, Tabasco sauce and cream cheese. Cook until cheese is melted and sauce is heated through. Serve at once.

Makes 4 servings.

Crookneck squash is a summer squash. Summer squash is harvested while still immature, when the entire squash is tender and edible. Varieties include the yellow crookneck, the large yellow straightneck, the greenish-white patty pan, the slender green zucchini and Italian marrow. Today some of these are imported and available year-round. Winter squash are marketed only when fully mature, and usually only the flesh is eaten. Some of the most important varieties are the acorn, butternut, buttercup, hubbard, golden delicious, spaghetti and banana. Winter squash varieties are most plentiful from early fall until late winter.

Green Chile Rice

My wife Millie got this recipe from a lady in her quilt guild. It has been served here in Roswell for many years and is great way to prepare an old standard. Try it.

1 cup of long grain white rice, cooked and drained (Do not use instant rice.)
1 stick of unsalted butter or margarine, softened
1 4-ounce can New Mexico green chiles, drained and chopped or 3 to 5 fresh or frozen green chiles, roasted, peeled, seeded, de-veined and chopped
16 ounces fresh dairy sour cream
1 pound of Monterey Jack cheese, shredded

1. Preheat oven to 350°F (175°C).
2. In a mixing bowl, combine cooked rice, butter or margarine, chiles and sour cream.
3. In a 9 x 13-inch casserole dish, place ½ of the rice mixture and cover with ½ of the cheese.
4. Add remaining rice mixture and cover with remaining cheese. Bake for 35 or 40 minutes.

Serves 4.

Marinated Onions

Simple and easy, this can be prepared a day ahead of time. The blue cheese is a nice contrast to the onions spiked with green chiles.

3 large red onions
½ cup vegetable oil
2 tablespoons lemon juice
1 4-ounce can New Mexico green chiles, drained and chopped
    or 3 to 5 fresh or frozen green chiles, roasted, peeled, seeded,
    de-veined and chopped
½ teaspoon garlic salt
½ teaspoon salt
½ teaspoon paprika
½ teaspoon sugar
¼ cup crumbled blue cheese

1. Place red onions in a large bowl.
2. In a cup, combine remaining ingredients except cheese. Stir well and pour over onions. Toss to coat.
3. Sprinkle cheese over onions; mix together. Cover and refrigerate 24 to 36 hours.

Makes 4 to 6 servings.

From a small gathering of 13 balloons in 1972, the Albuquerque International Balloon Fiesta has grown to become hands-down the largest balloon event in the world. Held each year during the first week in October, the Balloon Fiesta attracts over 700 balloons, over 1,000 pilots and tens of thousands of spectators. The Balloon Fiesta is unusual because the spectators get to mingle right on the launch field with the pilots and chase crews. This is definitely a sport that encourages spectator participation! But watch out for balloons taking off and landing. It's a little like herding cats when a hot air balloon lifts off. They go with the breeze, pilots navigating by ascending or descending into winds headed in different directions. The "Albuquerque Box," a rare layering of air currents that happens in few places—Albuquerque among them—sometimes lets balloonists take off, enjoy a spectacular flight, and land right back at the Balloon Fiesta Park. Prevailing lower winds blow south for takeoff, with northern moving winds a few hundred feet up, creating the "Box" that moves the balloons back to the park.

Peanut-Stuffed Acorn Squash

I love squash, and this rich, full-flavored dish makes the lowly squash a gourmet food. I make it every time I have some left over baked ham.

2 acorn squash, cut in half with seeds removed
2 tablespoons butter
2 cups minced baked ham
2 tablespoons white onion, minced
1 tablespoon packed brown sugar
1 tablespoon grated orange peel
¼ cup orange juice
1 teaspoon salt
1½ cups chopped unsalted Valencia peanuts
½ cup melted butter
½ cup packed brown sugar
½ cup unsalted Valencia peanuts

1. Preheat oven to 350°F (175°C). Lightly grease a shallow baking pan.
2. Place squashes cut side down on prepared pan. Bake 45 minutes, or until tender.
3. Remove from oven and scoop pulp into a bowl, leaving a thin shell intact.
4. In a large skillet, heat 2 tablespoons butter; sauté ham and onion. Stir in squash pulp, brown sugar, orange peel, orange juice and salt. Stir in 1 cup of the peanuts.
5. Fill squash shells with ham and squash mixture. Drizzle tops with melted butter; sprinkle with brown sugar and the remaining peanuts.
6. Place filled squash shells on a baking pan and return to oven. Bake 20 to 30 minutes until thoroughly heated.

Makes 4 servings

Many Americans are unfamiliar with Valencia peanuts. They are grown mostly here in New Mexico. Unlike most peanuts, they generally have three and sometimes 4 kernels inside each shell. Many believe their unique sweet flavor makes these the best tasting peanuts available.

Refried Pinto Beans

Refried beans are an integral part of New Mexico cooking, because they are nutritious, economical and delicious. The name "refried" should not be taken literally; one frying is all that is needed if it is thorough enough. Refried Beans is New Mexico's most popular side dish and keeps well when refrigerated.

1 pound dry pinto beans
6 to 8 cups distilled water
1 or 2 medium-size white onions, chopped
½ to 1 cup hot bacon drippings, lard or butter
salt

1. Thoroughly wash and drain beans; discard any foreign material.
2. In a 3-quart pan, combine beans, distilled water and onions. Soak overnight.
3. Discard soaking water. Cover with fresh distilled water and bring to a boil, cover and simmer, adding more water as needed. Cook for about 3 hours or until beans are very tender.
4. Drain and mash with potato masher or electric mixer, adding bacon drippings, lard or butter. Mix well.
5. Place mixture in a 10-inch fry pan. Cook and stir frequently, until beans are thickened and fat is absorbed.
Salt to taste.

Makes 5 or 6 cups.

El Morro National Monument is located 58 miles southeast of Gallup on NM 53 on an ancient east-west trail. The main feature of this national monument is a great sandstone promontory with a pool of water at its base. This pool of water never goes dry, no matter how hot the summer or how long since the last rain. As a shaded oasis in the western U.S. desert, this outcropping of rock has seen many centuries of travelers leave their signatures carved or written on it. It was called "A'ts'ina" (place of writings on the rock) by the Zuni Indians long before the Spanish explorers named it "El Morro" (the headland). Here in New Mexico it is frequently referred to as "Inscription Rock."

Spanish Rice

Another popular side dish and a staple in New Mexico cuisine, this is sometimes called Mexican or Red Rice. I sometimes use this as a stuffing for wild game birds or pork chops.

3 slices lean bacon
1 cup long-grain white rice
1 8-ounce can tomatoes, crushed, with liquid
½ cup chopped white onion
½ cup chopped red bell peppers
1 4-ounce can New Mexico green chiles, drained and chopped
    or 3 to 5 fresh or frozen green chiles, roasted, peeled, seeded,
    de-veined and chopped
⅛ teaspoon dried-leaf oregano
1 teaspoon salt
1 teaspoon red chile powder
1 10¾-ounce can chicken broth
1 6-ounce can tomato puree or paste
2 tablespoons olive oil
fresh cilantro, for garnish

1. In a heavy 2-quart pot, fry bacon until crisp. Remove bacon from pan, crumble and save for another dish.
2. Fry rice in bacon drippings until brown, stirring constantly. Add tomatoes, onion, bell peppers, green chiles, oregano, salt and red chile powder. Mix well.
3. Add chicken broth and tomato puree. Cover and cook until liquid is absorbed and rice is tender, about 5 minutes.
4. Transfer to serving bowl and sprinkle with olive oil and cilantro.

Makes 6 servings.

New Mexico's large Latino population is part of the second-largest and the fastest-growing minority group in the country. Over 30 million Hispanics live in the US, making up more than 12% of the population (US Census Bureau). By the year 2050, an estimated 97 million Hispanics will constitute 25 percent of the US population.

CHILI

There is no question that one of New Mexico's major contributions to American cuisine is chili. No one knows for sure who first combined meat and chile peppers, the main ingredients of chili. Some New Mexicans claim it was a chuckwagon cook who ran out of pepper. Others claim that, long ago, the Indians had discovered the anti-oxidative quality that chiles possess and sprinkled them on meat before drying to make jerky. At any rate, the combination of meat and chiles in innumerable combinations comprise what we now enjoy as chili.

When I visit chili cookoffs in the Southwest, I find a group of fun-loving folks who cut across ethnic and economic lines. They graciously share their love of chili with anyone willing to stop and sample their culinary efforts. They believe, as I do, that the best chili requires the perfect melding of flavor and heat. In the following recipes I have included some that are simple and easy to prepare as well as those that could be entered into a chili contest.

Remember –chile spelled with an "e" is a variety of pepper; chili spelled with an "i" refers to a mixture of meats, spices and chiles. In Texas, if you put beans in your chili they run you out of the state. Here in New Mexico, we are not so fussy; ubiquitous beans are often found in some of our chili recipes.

Albuquerque Oktoberfest Chili

The chili cookoff is a regular part of many Oktoberfest celebrations here in the West. At the Albuquerque cookoff, I met a great cook who was willing to share this recipe.

⅓ cup olive or vegetable oil
3 pounds lean beef, cut into 1-inch cubes
2 onions, finely chopped
3 garlic cloves, finely chopped
4 cups boiling water
1 teaspoon caraway seeds
2 teaspoons sesame seeds
½ teaspoon ground dried-leaf oregano
1 tablespoon ground hot red chile powder
2 tablespoons ground mild red chile powder
1 cup pitted olives
2 16-ounce cans kidney beans, drained
salt and pepper to taste

1. Heat olive oil in a 6-quart Dutch oven or heavy pot over medium heat. Add beef cubes, a few at a time, stirring to brown evenly. As beef browns remove from pan and set aside. After all beef is browned, add onions and garlic to pan and cook until soft.
2. Return beef to pan and season with salt. Add boiling water, caraway seeds, sesame seeds and oregano. Bring to a boil, reduce heat and simmer uncovered.
3. Slowly add ground chile, tasting until you get the degree of hotness and flavor you prefer.
4. Add olives and simmer uncovered for an additional 45 minutes to an hour. Taste and adjust seasonings as necessary. Add kidney beans and heat thoroughly.

Makes 6 servings.

Christopher Columbus is credited with the "discovery" of chile peppers on his first voyage to the New World. No one actually knows where chiles originated. It is generally accepted that they came from South America. Here in New Mexico they were prized for their amazing preservative and antioxidant qualities by the Native Americans.

Championship Chili

This recipe is a proven winner of chili cookoffs. Give it your own touch and enter one yourself. You can experiment but remember, you will be judged on flavor, texture of meat, consistency, blend of spices, aroma and color.

¾ cup all-purpose flour
1 tablespoon salt
½ teaspoon ground black pepper
1 pound lean pork shoulder, cut into ½ inch cubes
2 pounds lean beef shoulder, cut into ½ inch cubes
3 teaspoons vegetable oil
3 onions, chopped
6 garlic cloves, minced
6 cups beef broth
4 dried chipotle chiles
4 mild, fresh New Mexico green chiles, peeled, roasted, seeded,
    de-veined and chopped
ground cumin and salt to taste.
¼ cup water

1. Combine flour, salt and black pepper in a paper bag; add meat to bag and shake to coat. Save remaining flour.
2. Place oil in Dutch oven or heavy pot. Heat oil to high temperature until oil smokes. Add meat, stirring constantly to prevent sticking.
3. Add onions and garlic; cook until soft. Add beef broth and bring to a boil.
4. Wash chipotle chiles under cold running water. Remove stems and seeds and de-vein. Place in a saucepan and cover with water. Boil 5 minutes, then steep for 10 to 15 minutes.
5. Remove chiles with slotted spoon; puree in a food processor with 1½ cups of cooking water.
6. Stir puree into meat pot; add New Mexico chiles. Cover and simmer for 2 to 3 hours or until meat is tender. Add cumin and salt to taste.
7. Mix reserved flour from bag with ¼ cup cold water. Stir into chili and cook 3 to 5 minutes to thicken.

Makes about 8 servings.

Chicken & White Bean Chili

I use white Aztec beans when I make this chili, but they are hard to find outside New Mexico. The Great Northern bean will work as well. This unusual recipe is worth trying.

¼ cup butter
1 large white onion, chopped
1 garlic clove, finely chopped
4 cups cooked chicken, cut into 1-inch cubes
3 cups chicken broth
2 tablespoons fresh, chopped cilantro
1 tablespoon dried-leaf basil
2 teaspoons dried ground red chile
2 16-ounce cans white or Great Northern beans, drained
¾ cup chopped tomato
Tortilla chips.

1. In a 4-quart Dutch oven or heavy pot, heat butter; add onion and garlic; cook until soft.
2. Add remaining ingredients except for tomato and tortilla chips
3. Bring to a boil and reduce heat. Cover and simmer 1 hour, stirring occasionally.

Top with tomatoes and serve with tortilla chips.

Makes 6 servings.

Chili Colorado

Traditional chili with a modern spice treatment for a different flavor. Distinctive, warm and unusual, this recipe was given to me by a great cook, who loves to fool around with spices.

4 ounces dried red New Mexico chiles
3 cups water
½ cup olive or vegetable oil
2 large white onions, chopped
3 garlic cloves, minced
5 pounds boneless chuck, cut into 1-inch cubes
½ cup all-purpose flour
1 14½-ounce can beef broth
¼ cup fresh cilantro, chopped
2 teaspoons each of ground cumin, ground cloves, dried-leaf
    Mexican oregano, tarragon and rosemary
2 28-ounce cans tomatoes

1. Rinse chiles; discard stems and seeds. Break chiles into pieces. In a 2½-quart saucepan, combine chile pieces with water. Over high heat, bring to a boil; reduce heat, cover and simmer, until chiles are soft, about 30 minutes.
2. In a blender or food processor, puree chiles with their liquid. Rub puree though a fine strainer and discard residue.
3. Heat oil in a 6 to 8-quart Dutch oven or heavy pot over medium heat. Add onions and garlic and cook, stirring often, until onions are soft. Place flour in a small paper bag: add pork cubes and shake to coat with flour. Add meat and puree to pan and cook, stirring, 5 minutes.
4. Add broth, cilantro, cumin, cloves, oregano, tarragon, rosemary and tomatoes with their liquid. Reduce heat and simmer, uncovered, stirring often until meat is very tender, 3 to 4 hours.

Makes 8 servings.

When I first moved here to Roswell I worked at a large bus manufacturing plant. There I met many great Hispanic cooks who shared recipes with me when they learned of my love for this cuisine. One of my special friends, Mary Chavez. was good enough to share this chili recipe with me.

Cowpoke Chili

Still served today by chuckwagon cooks, this old standard is not for the faint of heart. If you like your chili hot, here is what you are looking for.

1 pound slab bacon
2 pounds dry pinto beans or navy beans
1 large white onion, sliced
4 garlic cloves, sliced
12 cups distilled water
1 16-ounce can tomatoes
2 ancho chile peppers, roasted, peeled, seeded and de-veined
2 serrano chile peppers, roasted, peeled, seeded and de-veined
2½ teaspoons salt
1 teaspoon coriander seeds, crushed
12 canned serrano peppers

1. Remove rind from bacon. Cut rind into ½ inch squares. Cut bacon into small pieces and set aside.
2. Put rind, beans, onions and garlic into a kettle. Add water and bring to a boil. Lower heat, cover and cook beans gently about 1½ hours.
3. Uncover and cook 15 additional minutes. Skim off the fat.
4. In a separate pan, fry reserved bacon pieces until slightly crisp. Add tomatoes and remaining ingredients to bacon. Cook over medium heat about 10 minutes. Skim off fat.
5. Add bacon and tomato mixture to beans. Continue cooking over low heat about 1 hour, or until beans are tender.

Makes about 6 servings.

Although the atmosphere on the cattle trail was rowdy at times, even the greenest of cowhands understood what was acceptable and not acceptable around the chuckwagon. Riders approaching the campsite knew better than to stir up dust that could blow into the food or to park their horses too close to camp.

Gringo Chili

Quick and easy to fix, this mild chili is a good way for those unfamiliar with this dish to get acquainted. Try it, and find out what all the excitement is about.

2 teaspoons vegetable oil
½ medium white onion, coarsely chopped
1 pound lean beef, coarsely ground
1 tablespoon mild ground red chile
1 4-ounce can mild New Mexico green chiles, drained and chopped
   or 3 to 5 fresh or frozen mild green chiles, roasted, peeled,
   seeded, de-veined and chopped
¼ teaspoon dried-leaf oregano
¾ teaspoon ground cumin
2 garlic cloves, finely chopped
2 10½-ounce cans tomato soup
1 10½-ounce can onion soup
1 16-ounce can pinto beans, drained

1. In a large Dutch oven or heavy pot, heat oil. Add onion and cook until soft.
2. Combine meat with ground chile, green chiles, oregano, cumin and garlic. Add to pot and break up with fork as mixture cooks. Stir frequently and cook until meat is brown.
3. Add tomato soup, onion soup, and pinto beans. Bring to a boil; reduce heat and simmer, uncovered, until chili mixture thickens to desired consistency.

Makes 4 servings.

"Gringo" is a term in the Spanish language used in some countries of Latin America to refer to foreigners from different cultures, especially from the Untied States. Some disagreement exists among English speakers regarding whether or not gringo is a derogatory term. It sometimes does carry derogatory, paternalistic or even endearing connotations, depending on the context and the intent of the user.

Jose's Fast Chili

Jose's RT66 Fast Food Diner is gone, but the memory of the old railroad-car diner is brought alive with this, his special chili. Quick and easy to prepare.

3 tablespoons vegetable oil
1 pound course ground beef
1 large white onion, finely chopped
2½ cups cooked or canned pinto beans
1 15-ounce can tomato sauce
1 teaspoon salt
1 tablespoons all-purpose flour
2½ teaspoons Chili Powder (See below.)
3 tablespoons water

Chile Powder
7 tablespoons ground red chili powder
2 tablespoons garlic powder
1½ tablespoons ground cumin
1½ tablespoons ground dry-leaf oregano, regular or Mexican variety

1. Heat oil in a large skillet, and cook meat until slightly brown.
2. Add onion, and cook until soft.
3. Add beans, un-drained, and tomato sauce. Cook over medium heat 15 minutes. Stir frequently.
4. In separate bowl, combine salt, flour, chili powder and water. Add mixture to meat and cover. Simmer 1 hour, stirring occasionally.

Makes 6 servings

Try making your own chili powder using the above ratio of ingredients. Using various types of dried chiles, such as dried green chile powder, can give you unusual taste treats.

West of the Pecos Chili

Lean and mean, this is a chili for those who like it hot. Novices need not bother with this one.

3 tablespoons vegetable oil
2 pounds lean beef, cut in 1-inch cubes
½ cup red chile powder
2 teaspoons salt
2 tablespoons ground dry-leaf oregano
1 tablespoon cayenne pepper
4 garlic cloves, minced
8 cups beef stock or broth
½ cup masa harina or cornmeal
½ cup cold water

1. Heat oil in a large Dutch oven or heavy pot over medium heat.
2. Add beef, about 1 pound at a time, and brown, stirring constantly. Remove each pound after it browns.
3. Return browned beef to pot. Add seasonings and beef stock or broth. Cover and simmer 1½ to 2 hours. Skim off the excess fat.
4. Combine masa harina or cornmeal with cold water and stir into chili. Simmer an additional 30 minutes.

Makes 6 servings.

Mom's Simple Chili

I was raised in Colorado, and here's the quick and easy way my mother made chili. This is a good way to acquire a taste for this popular offering.

2 pounds coarsely ground chuck
4 tablespoons of Chile Powder (See page 190) or your favorite chili
   powder mix
2 garlic cloves, chopped
4 tablespoons all-purpose flour
4 tablespoons vegetable oil
1 white onion chopped
1 teaspoon salt
4 cups hot water

1. In a medium-size bowl, mix together meat, chili powder, garlic and flour.
2. In a large heavy skillet, heat oil over medium heat; add onion and sauté until tender.
3. Add meat mixture to skillet and cook until meat is browned. Add salt.
4. Slowly add water; cover and simmer 1 hour or until tender.

Makes 4 servings

My grandparents were homesteaders in Colorado's early days. The Homestead Act (signed into law by President Abraham Lincoln on May 20, 1862) was a United States federal law that gave freehold title to 160-acre-parcels (one-quarter section) of undeveloped land outside of the original 13 colonies. To gain ownership of a parcel of land, one had to live on the land for five years, making improvements and showing land use, such as cultivation. Anyone, including freed slaves, who had never taken up arms against the U.S. Government (a restriction that barred those who fought for the Confederacy in the Civil War!) could follow these procedures and become a landowner.

Eventually 1.6 million homesteads were granted and 270 million acres were privatized between 1862 and 1964, a total of 10% of all lands in the United States. Unfortunately, much of this land fell into the hands of speculators, railroads and timber interests, and the law was repealed in 1977.

New Mexico Green Chili (Chili Verde)

When you go into a New Mexico restaurant and order chile, the waitperson will ask you, "Red or Green?" If you say green, chances are this is what you will be served.

2 tablespoons vegetable oil
⅓ cup all-purpose flour
3 pounds lean boneless pork shoulder, cut into ½-inch cubes
3 white onions, coarsely chopped
2 16-ounce cans whole New Mexico green chiles, drained, seeded and cut into 2-inch slices.
2 16-ounce cans whole tomatoes
3 cups water
2 teaspoons salt
½ teaspoon dried-leaf oregano

1. In a heavy skillet, heat oil. Place flour in a small paper bag; add pork cubes and shake to coat with flour. Add coated pork to oil, a few cubes at a time, and brown evenly. Remove pork and place in a 5-quart Dutch oven or heavy pot.
2. Add onions and garlic to skillet and cook until soft stirring occasionally. Remove from heat and add to Dutch oven with browned pork.
3. Stir all remaining ingredients into the Dutch oven with the pork. Bring mixture to a boil, reduce heat and cook uncovered, about 45 minutes. Taste and adjust seasonings. Cook an additional ½-hour longer.

Makes 6 servings.

The International Chili Society defines Chili Verde as any kind of meat or combination of meats cooked with green chile peppers, various spices and other ingredients—with the exception of beans and pasta, which are strictly forbidden. The International Chili Society (ICS) is a non-profit organization that sanctions chili cookoffs' judging, cooking rules and regulations. All winners of ICS sanctioned cookoffs qualify to compete for cash prizes and awards at the World's Championship Chili Cookoff held each year in October. The ICS is the largest food contest and festival organization in the world.

Rio Grande Red

This a good example of red chile. Hot and hearty, it is the kind of chili that warms your tummy and makes you come back for more.

2 tablespoons vegetable oil
1 large white onion, coarsely chopped
3 pounds lean coarsely ground beef
3 garlic cloves, finely chopped
4 tablespoons ground hot red chile peppers
4 tablespoons ground mild red chile peppers
2 teaspoons ground cumin
3 cups water
1½ teaspoons salt, or to taste

1. Heat oil in large Dutch oven or large heavy pot over medium heat. Add onion and cook until soft.
2. Combine the meat, garlic, ground chile and cumin. Add meat and spice mixture to pot. Break up lumps with a fork; cook, stirring occasionally, until meat is browned.
3. Stir in water and salt. Bring to a boil; reduce heat and simmer uncovered about 2½ hours. Stir mixture occasionally; cook until meat is tender and flavors are well blended. Add more water as necessary.

Makes 6 servings.

Every year in Ruidoso, New Mexico, hundreds of people gather to witness and experience a little taste of the Old West at the Chuckwagon Cookoff. The weekend kicks off with the "Authentic Chuckwagon" competition. Contestants unveil their historically accurate chuckwagons to be judged. Then as the sun comes up, the fires get started. What follows is a contest of cowboy cooking over a fire pit that in the end will crown the one true "Cookie." Contestants come from all over the region and range from real rope-slinging cowboys to restaurant chefs. The results are often surprising, with lots of fun times and great eating for all.

Sweet Chili

Many folks prefer sweet chili. I think this is as good a sweet chili gets—tasty, warm and rich.

1 pound lean ground beef
1 large white onion, minced
1 8-ounce can tomato sauce
1 cup Refried Beans (See page 28), or 1 16-ounce can
1 cup kidney beans, or 1 16-ounce can, drained
1 cup water
¼ cup finely chopped celery
¼ cup green or red bell pepper, finely chopped
¼ teaspoon hot red chile powder
salt and black pepper to taste
1 teaspoon paprika
⅛ teaspoon garlic salt
2 teaspoons mild chili powder
¼ teaspoon Worcestershire sauce
⅛ teaspoon prepared mustard
½ teaspoon brown sugar
½ teaspoon molasses

1. In a Dutch oven or heavy 6-quart pan, brown meat and onion and drain off fat.
2. Combine remaining ingredients and simmer for at least 2 hours.

Makes 4 servings

Vegetarian Chili

For those who don't want meat in their chili, here is the best meatless chili I have found. I also find a number of uses for leftovers of this versatile dish.

1 undrained 28-ounce can crushed tomatoes
2 medium white onions, chopped
2 medium zucchini (2½ cups), halved lengthwise and sliced
1 16-ounce can red kidney beans, rinsed
1 tablespoon chili powder
1 15-ounce can garbanzo beans, rinsed
1 teaspoon ground cumin
1 12-to-14-ounce can hominy
¾ teaspoon garlic powder
1 6-ounce can tomato paste
½ teaspoon sugar
2 4-ounce cans diced New Mexico green chiles
2 cups vegetable broth
salt to taste
2 cups Monterey Jack cheese, shredded
dairy sour cream
fresh cilantro

1. In a Dutch oven or heavy pot, combine all ingredients except cheese.
2. Heat to boiling; reduce heat. Simmer, covered for 30 minutes.
3. Remove from heat and add cheese; stir until melted. Salt to taste.
Serve with dairy sour cream and garnish with cilantro if desired.

Makes 8 servings.

Quick and Easy Chili with Beans

Full-flavored and rich tasting, this is one of the best easy-to-fix chilis I have found. You must try this one.

¼ cup vegetable oil
3 pounds lean coarsely ground beef
2 jalapeño peppers, stems removed, seeded and chopped
2 medium white onions, chopped
2 garlic cloves, crushed
3 16-ounce cans whole tomatoes
2 tablespoons chili powder
2 teaspoons crushed cumin seeds
¼ teaspoon Tabasco sauce
1 cup water
3 15-ounce cans pinto or kidney beans, undrained

1. In a large Dutch oven or heavy pot, heat oil. Cook beef, jalapeño peppers, onions and garlic until beef is lightly brown.
2. Add all remaining ingredients, except beans. Cover and simmer for 45 minutes.
3. Stir in undrained beans. Cover and simmer 25 minutes.

Makes 4 servings.

When you find you have a mouthfull of a 4-alarm chile, don't wait for the fire department to put out the fire! Simply reach for a glass of milk and swish it around in your mouth. Among the other remedies are sour cream, olive oil, peanut butter or buttermilk. Have one of these handy when you try out a new recipe that calls for the use of New Mexico chiles.

SAUCES

The heart—some say the soul—of New Mexico cooking is its sauces. When you first visit a New Mexico restaurant, as you order you will be asked "Red or Green." Your waiter or waitress is asking if you prefer red or green sauce on your meal. I know of nowhere in the country where sauces play as important role as they do here in the Land of Enchantment. Sauces: One could say that sauces represent the personality of our cooking, providing both flavor and accent.

I'm sure I could write a book on the infinite variety of sauces that are prepared in this state. I offer a few choice ones here, and I think you be pleasantly surprised to see just how much they vary. Sauces from mild to hot are included, along with basic ones that you can embellish as you choose. You can modify these sauces to suit specific dishes they are created for and to appeal to individual tastes. You can also vary their heat by the hotness of the chiles or chile powder you decide to use.

Almond Red Sauce

You can control the heat level of this savory sauce easily by simply increasing or decreasing the amount and type of chile used.

½ cup toasted slivered almonds
2 tablespoons vegetable oil
1 cup finely chopped white onions
1 garlic clove, crushed
1 8-ounce can tomato sauce
2 teaspoons paprika
1 teaspoon ground red New Mexico chile
¼ teaspoon ground chili powder

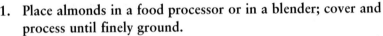

1. Place almonds in a food processor or in a blender; cover and process until finely ground.
2. In a small skillet, heat oil over medium heat. Add onion and garlic; stir frequently until onion is tender.
3. Stir in remaining ingredients, except for the almonds. Heat to a boil; reduce heat. Simmer 1 minute, stirring constantly. Stir in almonds. Serve hot. This full-bodied sauce is especially good with beef or pork.

Makes about 1-3/4 cups.

Ancho Mole Sauce

No New Mexico cookbook would be complete without a mole sauce, and here is an excellent one. Ancho chiles are the dried, mild poblano chiles frequently used in mole sauces. These sauces are often referred to in Spanish by the more specific name Mole Poblano.

2 dried New Mexico red chiles, seeded and stems removed
2 ancho dried chiles, seeded and stems removed
1 small white onion, chopped
1 garlic clove, chopped
1 medium tomato, peeled, seeded and chopped
¼ cup almonds, blanched
¼ cup corn tortillas, cut in pieces
⅛ teaspoon ground coriander
⅛ teaspoon ground cloves
⅛ teaspoon ground cinnamon
¼ cup raisins
1½ tablespoons vegetable oil
½ cup chicken broth
1 ounce unsweetened chocolate

1. In a food processor or blender, combine all ingredients except vegetable oil, chicken broth and chocolate. Puree until mixture is smooth.
2. Heat oil in skillet and sauté the puree about 10 minutes at medium heat, stirring frequently. Add chicken broth and chocolate. Cook until sauce thickens.

Makes about 1 cup.

Basic Green Sauce

Versatile and full flavored, this green sauce can be used on many New Mexico dishes. If you have been looking for a versatile green sauce, you just found a great one.

2 tablespoons vegetable oil
1 large white onion, finely chopped
1 green jalapeño chile, seeded and finely chopped
6 New Mexico green chiles, roasted, peeled, seeded and finely
    chopped (about ½ cup)
1 garlic clove, finely minced
½ cup whipping cream
¼ teaspoon salt

1. In a skillet, heat oil and add onion, chiles and garlic. Cook over medium heat, stirring occasionally, until onion is tender, about 6 to 8 minutes.
2. Place in small serving bowl and stir in whipping cream.
Can be used warm or cold

Makes about 1⅓ cups.

Basic Red Sauce

Here is a sauce that can be used for a number of dishes. It freezes well; I simply double the recipe and freeze the extra sauce in ice cube trays. Then I use the cubes as needed.

8 dried, mild New Mexico red chiles
3½ cups warm water
¼ cup vegetable oil
½ cup white onion, chopped
2 garlic cloves, chopped
1 tablespoon Mexican oregano (dried-leaf will do if Mexican is
   not available)
1 tablespoon cumin seeds
1 teaspoon salt

1. In a bowl, cover dry chiles with warm water. Let stand for about
   30 minutes or until softened.
2. Strain chiles and reserve liquid. Remove stems and seeds and de-
   vein. Set aside.
3. In a 2-quart saucepan, heat oil. Add onion and garlic; stir until
   onion is tender. Stir in chiles, 2 cups of reserved liquid and the
   remaining ingredients.
4. Heat to boiling; reduce heat. Simmer uncovered 20 minutes; cool.
5. Pour into a food processor or blender; cover and purée. Rub
   purée through fine strainer and discard residue. Cover and
   refrigerate up to 10 days or freeze.

Makes 2½ cups.

Chipotle Chile Sauce

The smoky sweet flavor of the chipotle pepper gives this sauce a subtle, deep heat with chocolate overtones. The chipotle is the smoked and dried red jalapeño chile pepper. Because its flavor is concentrated, it is hotter than a fresh green jalapeño, so be careful!

2 dried chipotle chiles
2 slices bacon, diced
¼ cup finely chopped white onion
1 cup beef broth
3 cups finely chopped tomatoes
¼ cup finely chopped carrot
¼ cup finely chopped celery
¼ cup flopped fresh cilantro
¼ teaspoon black pepper
½ teaspoon salt

1. Cover chiles with warm water. Let stand about 1 hour, until softened. Drain and finely chop. If you like it hot, leave veins and seeds.
2. In a 2-quart saucepan, cook and stir bacon and onion until bacon is crisp; stir in chiles and remaining ingredients. Cook until vegetables are tender.
3. Pour into a food processor or blender and purée. Rub purée through fine strainer and discard residue. Place in glass dish, cover and refrigerate until ready to use.

Makes about 4 cups.

Enchilada Sauce

Another sauce no New Mexico cook's repertoire should ever be without, enchilada sauce creates one of the most popular meals in our state. This old version has stood the test of time and will win compliments whenever you serve it.

2 tablespoons butter
2 garlic cloves, minced
6 tablespoons mild red chili powder
1 14½-ounce can plum tomatoes
2 tablespoons tomato paste
1 cup chicken stock
1 cup water
¼ teaspoon salt
⅛ teaspoon black pepper
½ cup fresh cilantro, finely minced

1. In a 1½ or 2 quart saucepan, heat butter; add garlic and sauté over medium heat 1 to 2 minutes.
2. Reduce heat to low and stir in chili powder. Cook stirring constantly, 2 to 3 minutes to remove raw chile taste. Watch carefully because chili powder burns very easily. Remove from heat.
3. Mash tomatoes with fork. Add tomatoes, tomato paste, chicken stock and water to saucepan. Simmer at low heat, stirring frequently, for 10 minutes.
4. Taste and adjust salt and pepper to taste. Stir in cilantro after cooking is complete. Sauce may be used immediately or refrigerated 3 to 4 days. It may be frozen for longer storage.

Makes about 2½ cups.

Hot Citrus Barbecue Sauce

This is an excellent sauce for use with fish. I like to cook trout over a fire in aluminum foil. At the last minute, I open the foil, brush this sauce on both sides of the trout and rewrap in foil. Then I cook it for another 2 minutes per side.

1 tablespoon vegetable oil
1 large white onion, finely chopped
1 tablespoon ground red New Mexico chiles
¼ teaspoon chili powder
1 jalapeño pepper, seeded, de-veined and chopped
1 cup orange juice
2 tablespoons sugar
½ cup lime juice
2 tablespoon lemon juice
1 teaspoon salt
1 tablespoon snipped fresh cilantro

1. In a skillet, heat oil; add onion, ground chiles, chili powder and jalapeño pepper. Stirring frequently, cook over medium heat until onion is tender, about 5 minutes.
2. Stir in remaining ingredients and heat to a rolling boil; reduce heat to low.
3. Simmer uncovered about 10 minutes, stirring occasionally. Store in refrigerator.

Makes about 2⅓ cups.

Jalapeño Sauce

Here is a good example of Santa Fe style cooking. This unusual sauce is the specialty of one of Santa Fe's finest bed-and-breakfast inns.

6 tablespoons softened butter
2 red jalapeño peppers, finely chopped
6 ounces cream cheese
2 egg yolks
2 tablespoons lemon or lime juice
½ teaspoon salt

1. In a small saucepan, melt 2 tablespoons butter over low heat.
2. Add jalapeños and cook, stirring constantly, until softened (about 2 minutes).
3. In a medium bowl, combine the remaining 4 tablespoons of butter, cream cheese, egg yolks, lemon or lime juice and salt.
4. Add above mixture to sauce pan and cook, stirring constantly, until the sauce thickens, about 2 minutes. Do not allow sauce to boil. Remove to a glass bowl and cover. Refrigerate and warm to use.

Makes about a 1½ cups.

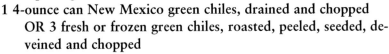

Taco Sauce

This sassy sauce can be served with any favorite dish. I like to double this recipe and freeze the extra in an ice cube tray for use later.

1 16-ounce can of tomatoes, undrained
1 large white onion, minced
2 garlic cloves, crushed
1½ tablespoons oil of choice
1 teaspoon dried leaf oregano
¾ teaspoon ground cumin
¾ teaspoon ground coriander
1 4-ounce can New Mexico green chiles, drained and chopped
   OR 3 fresh or frozen green chiles, roasted, peeled, seeded, de-
   veined and chopped
1 tablespoon tomato paste
1½ teaspoons sugar
1 teaspoon fresh cilantro, chopped
1 teaspoon white vinegar
salt and black pepper to taste

1. In a blender or food processor, coarsely puree the tomatoes with their juice.
2. In a large skillet, cook onion and garlic in oil over medium heat until onion is soft.
3. Add oregano, cumin, and ground coriander for 2 minutes stirring gently.
4. Add the tomato puree (from step 1), chopped green chiles, tomato paste, sugar, cilantro and vinegar.
5. Simmer for15 minutes, stirring often until mixture thickens. Salt and pepper to taste.

Makes 2 cups.

Salsas

Today, more salsa than ketchup is sold in the United States. Everyone has a favorite brand or version of a fresh or uncooked salsa. Don't believe the commercials that claim the best salsa is always made in Texas! New Mexico cafés were serving salsa long before it became the rage in other states.

Salsas add a refreshing combination of flavors that can enhance the blandest of foods. They also add a delightful texture of their own. Serve them warm or chilled—the choice is yours. I have included a couple fruit salsas to show you how easily you can incorporate fruits into your salsa offerings; try my Apple or Pineapple Salsas.

Apple Salsa

I love apples and make sure I eat at least an apple a day. With so many varieties now available at your local grocery store, it's easy to vary the taste of this simple salsa. Here I use the new Sonya from New Zealand, a wonderfully sweet relative of our Golden Delicious variety.

2 Sonya apples
2 tablespoons fresh lime juice
½ cup chopped orange segments
½ cup bell peppers, finely chopped
½ cup red onions, finely chopped
1 jalapeño pepper, seeded, stem removed and finely chopped
1 clove garlic, minced
2 tablespoons fresh cilantro, chopped
1 tablespoon cider vinegar
½ teaspoon cumin
1 teaspoon vegetable oil

1. Core and dice apples into ¼ inch pieces.
2. In glass bowl toss immediately with lime juice.
3. Stir in remaining ingredients. Chill for 2 hours before you serve. This salsa is especially good when served over fish or chicken.

Makes 6 servings.

Avocado Salsa

This is another use for one of my favorites, the avocado. I think an avocado tastes great, but outside of an occasional guacamole dip, few folks reach for this high-fiber food. Great for salads or as a side dish, the avocado is high in fat, but most of the fat is the heart-healthy monounsaturated kind. You'll also get protein, a good dose of vitamins A and E, some B vitamins, lots of potassium and a dollop of copper. The rich and creamy avocado has been called the "chocolate" of fruits (often thought of as a vegetable, the avocado is technically a fruit).

2 tomatoes, seeded and diced
¼ cup red onion, chopped
½ avocado, peeled and cubed
1 jalapeño pepper, seeded and chopped (less if you want!)
1 tablespoon snipped fresh cilantro
2 tablespoons red wine vinegar
2 teaspoons grated line zest
1 teaspoon fresh lime juice
¼ teaspoon ground cumin

1. In a non-reactive glass or plastic bowl, combine all ingredients. Let stand for 15 minutes.

Makes 4 servings.

Cantaloupe Salsa

Sweet and hot! This is a nice combination for the adventuresome and another new addition to the growing list of salsas, one you should give a try.

2 cups diced cantaloupe (cut into ¼-inch pieces)
¼ cup finely chopped sweet onion (such as Vidalia)
2 teaspoons fresh basil, finely chopped
1 jalapeño pepper, seeded and minced
1 tablespoon fresh lime juice
¼ teaspoon salt

1. In a non-reactive glass or plastic bowl, toss together all ingredients, cover and refrigerate for at least 15 minutes.

Makes 4 servings.

Corn Salsa

When fresh corn is in season, I like to cut it off the cob for making this light salsa, another use of the most common staple in our cuisine.

1 16-ounce can of kernel corn, drained or the corn cut from 6 fresh
    corn cobs
1 4-ounce can New Mexico green chiles, drained and chopped
    or 3 to 5 fresh or frozen green chiles, roasted, peeled, seeded,
    de-veined and chopped
1 jalapeño chile, seeded and finely chopped
¼ cup green, red or yellow bell pepper, stems removed, seeded
    and chopped
¼ cup green onions, sliced with some tops
2 tablespoons white-wine vinegar
1 tablespoon vegetable oil
salt, to taste

1.   In a serving bowl, mix together all ingredients.
2.   Cover and refrigerate until chilled, about 1 hour.

Makes about 2 cups.

Cucumber Salsa

Fresh and elegant, this urban salsa is served at many outdoor restaurants in New Mexico. Many salsas like this one can also be utilized as a dip and served with tortillas or specialty chips.

2 medium cucumbers, peeled, seeded and coarsely shredded
1 cup dairy sour cream
1 cup plain yogurt
¼ cup freshly chopped parsley
¼ cup freshly chopped cilantro
1 teaspoon ground cumin
salt to taste

1. In a small serving bowl, mix all ingredients.
2. Can be served at once or covered and refrigerated until ready for use.

Makes about 3 cups.

Since this salsa contains milk, you might try this technique to slow down the spoilage time if you will not be using it right away. Put a half-inch of water in a bowl that is slightly larger than your salsa bowl and place it in your freezer. When you are ready to serve the salsa, simply place the smaller salsa bowl on top of the ice in the larger bowl.

Fresh Tomato Salsa

If you grow your own tomatoes here is great way to use them. This is one of my personal favorites.

2 medium tomatoes, peeled and seeded
2 serrano chiles, peeled, seeded and de-veined
2 yellow wax chiles, peeled, seeded and de-veined
3 radishes, trimmed
3 cloves garlic
1 bunch of green onions, trimmed
    or ½ medium red onion, chopped
1 cup cilantro leaves
salt, to taste
1 tablespoon tomato paste
½ cup water

1. Coarsely chop the first seven ingredients. Pieces should be chunky, not minced. Place in a glass or plastic bowl.
2. In a cup, stir together salt, tomato paste, and water. Mix well.
3. Pour over chopped ingredients and mix well. Serve at once or refrigerate until chilled. This salsa can be refrigerated up to one week.

Makes 6 servings.

Picante Salsa

Here is a basic salsa you can use for a side dish on many meals. Easy to prepare and tasty, it should be prepared a day ahead of serving so flavors can blend.

3 medium tomatoes, seeded and chopped
1 green or red bell pepper, seeded, stem removed and chopped
½ cup white onion, chopped
1 jalapeño pepper, seeded, de-veined and finely chopped
2 tablespoons fresh cilantro, chopped
2 garlic cloves, minced
1½ tablespoons fresh lime juice
¼ teaspoon red chili powder
½ teaspoon ground cumin
½ teaspoon salt

1. In a large non-reactive glass or plastic bowl, combine all ingredients and mix well.
2. Refrigerate over night.

Makes 4 servings.

Tomatillo Salsa

Tart and snappy, this is an exciting blend of sweet and hot with just the right amount of acidity.

3 fresh or canned tomatillos
⅓ cup diced fresh pineapple
⅓ cup chopped red onion
¼ cup red or green bell pepper, stem removed, seeded and minced
2 tablespoons chopped fresh cilantro
3 tablespoons fresh orange juice
1½ tablespoon fresh lime juice
1 tablespoon white vinegar
1 garlic clove, minced
1½ teaspoons jalapeño, chipotle or other hot chile of choice, minced
salt and black pepper to taste.

1. Remove husks from fresh tomatillos; rinse and finely chop. Color should be bright green, not yellow, when skinned. If you use canned tomatillos, purée in food processor.
2, In a glass or plastic bowl, combine all ingredients. Cover and refrigerate until chilled.
Salsa may be stored in refrigerator for 3 days.

Makes 4 servings.

Winter Salsa

I have no idea why this is referred to as *winter* salsa. I have prepared it for years and have never grown tired of its lively taste.

1 cup cucumber, chopped, peeled and seeded
1½ cups tomato, chopped and seeded
1 cup red bell pepper, stem removed, seeded and chopped
½ cup chopped radishes
½ cup chopped red onion
3 tablespoons minced shallots
¼ cup minced cilantro
1 teaspoon jalapeño chile, seeded, de-veined and chopped
salt to taste
1 tablespoon fresh lime juice
2 tablespoons fresh orange juice

1. In a glass, plastic or other non-reactive bowl, combine all ingredients.
2. Marinate at room temperature at least 1 hour.

Makes 4 to 6 servings.

DESSERTS

While New Mexico cuisine is known mainly for its spices, it also offers a variety of tasty regional sweets. You will find cakes made unique by their use of local ingredients as well as some deserts traditionally associated with the Southwest such as Natillas. The treats in this chapter may not be spicy, but they certainly are tasty!

A mulberry tree at my grandparents' homestead ranch gives me one of my fondest memories. I used to eat mulberries until I was both blue and ill. When I moved to Roswell, I found a number of mulberry trees and best of all, a great recipe for Maple Mulberry Cake. Try it you and you will be pleasantly surprised. If you are unable to find the mulberries, use blueberries, which make an excellent substitute.

Pecans are now a major crop New Mexico and gaining in popularity all the time. We use pecans in many cakes, because they add a special taste and texture. Toasting them before using heightens their wonderful flavor. They are now almost as common in our dishes as they are in Southern cooking.

You are in for a treat the first time you try Capirotada. This version of Mexican bread pudding is worth the effort. The wine-soaked raisins make it delightfully sweet. Your family and guests will reward you with compliments when you serve this desert.

Apple Cake

Here is a great moist cake. I like simple cakes and of course I love apples. I like Granny Smith apples for cooking, but if you have another kind that you prefer, use it.

3 cups all-purpose flour
1 teaspoon baking powder
¼ teaspoon salt
1 tablespoon baking soda
1 tablespoon ground cinnamon
3 eggs
2 cups sugar
1 cup vegetable oil
2 teaspoons vanilla extract
4 unpeeled Granny Smith apples, cored and grated
1 cup pecans, chopped

1. Preheat oven to 350°F (175°C). Generously grease a 10-inch tube or bunt pan with shortening and flour.
2. In a medium-size bowl, sift together, flour, baking powder, salt, soda and cinnamon. Set aside.
3. In a large bowl, beat eggs; add sugar and beat well. Add oil and vanilla extract; beat well. Stir in dry ingredients.
4. Add apples to batter; stir well. Stir in pecans and pour into prepared cake pan. Bake for 1 hour or until stop springs back when touched.
5. Immediately turn out of pan onto a wire rack.

Makes 8 servings.

Biscuit Pudding

This modern-day chuckwagon dessert is rich and satisfying—and strictly New Mexican.

3 cups of day-old biscuit or bread crumbs
2 tablespoons butter
⅛ teaspoon ground cloves
1 cup packed brown sugar
1 cup water
¼ teaspoon ground cinnamon
1 cup (4 ounces) Cheddar cheese, shredded
1 cup dried apple slices
½ cup raisins
½ cup pecans, chopped
½ cup softened butter
sweetened whipped cream

1. Preheat oven to 300°F (145°C). Spread the crumbs in a shallow baking pan and lightly dot with 2 tablespoons of butter. Bake until golden brown.
2. In a small saucepan, combine cloves, brown sugar, water and ground cinnamon over medium heat, stirring constantly until sugar dissolves and becomes syrup.
3. In a 9-inch ungreased casserole dish, spread 1 cup of the browned crumbs. Pour ⅓ cup of the syrup over crumbs and sprinkle with cheese.
4. Add another cup of crumbs. Sprinkle on apples, raisins and pecans.
5. Top with another ⅓ cup of syrup and balance of crumbs; pour balance of syrup over the mixture.
6. Dot with remaining butter. Bake uncovered 25 to 30 minutes or until mixture bubbles.
7. Cool at least 15 minutes before serving. Top with sweetened whipped cream.

Makes 6 servings.

Capirotada

Madeira wine gives this delicate pudding a sophisticated taste. American-made Madeira is not as distinctive as the Portuguese or Spanish varieties, but its cost is a fraction of the price of the imports. Capirotada is usually served during lent.

½ cup raisins
1 cup Madeira or a sweet wine
12–14 slices day-old French bread
½ cup piñon nuts or pecans
2 cups sugar
3½ cups water
1 teaspoon ground cinnamon
5 tablespoons butter
1½ teaspoons vanilla extract
1 cup (4 ounces) shredded Jack or Longhorn cheese
whipped cream or ice cream

1. Place raisins in a bowl and cover with madeira; soak at least 20 minutes.
2. Preheat oven to 350°F (175°C). Butter a 13 x 9-inch baking dish.
3. Tear bread into bite-sized pieces, place in a shallow baking pan. Toast in oven 10 minutes.
4. Remove bread from oven. You can leave the oven on. In a mixing bowl, toss bread and piñon or pecan nuts.
5. Place sugar in a saucepan over medium-high heat, stirring constantly, until sugar melts and turns to a light caramel color. Add water and cinnamon; do this carefully as the hot syrup may splatter as you add the water.
6. Reduce heat and add butter. Drain raisins and add them and the vanilla extract. Continue stirring until butter has melted.
7. Pour bread mixture into prepared baking dish; mix in cheese. Pour syrup (from step 6) over all.
8. Bake in preheated oven for about 30 minutes at the same temperature as above.

Serve topped with whipped cream or ice cream.

Makes 6 to 8 servings.

Churros

An import from Spain and Mexico, churros are fast becoming a regular item in New Mexico cuisine. I fix these regularly, and like to dip them in my coffee or hot chocolate. In Mexico or Spain they are made with a tool called a *churrera*. Here they are usually made using a pastry bag with a large star tip.

2½ cups water
¼ cup dark brown sugar.
¼ cup vegetable oil of choice
½ teaspoon vanilla extract
½ teaspoon ground cinnamon
1 teaspoon salt
½ cup unsalted butter
2 cups all purpose flour
3 eggs
vegetable oil for frying.
¼ cup white sugar for topping

1. In a medium-size pot, combine first 7 ingredients. Bring to a boil. Stir in flour; remove from heat.
2. Move hot mixture to a mixing bowl and whisk in eggs, one at a time, until fully incorporated.
3. Allow dough to cool and then place in a pastry piping bag fitted with a large star tip.
4. Heat vegetable oil in a large skillet to 350°F (175°C). Squeeze 4-inch strips into hot oil. Fry 3 or 4 strips at a time until golden brown, turning once, about 2 minutes per side.
Drain on paper towels. Roll churros in sugar to coat.

Serves 4.

Maple Mulberry Cake

Makes sure you use fully ripe mulberries. Unripe berries are sour and inedible. If you can't find mulberries, use blueberries. Incidentally, ripe mulberries also make great wine.

¼ cup shortening
½ cup maple syrup
½ cup packed brown sugar
¾ cup dairy sour cream
2 eggs, beaten
1 cup ripe mulberries or blueberries.
2 cups all-purpose flour
1 teaspoon ground ginger
1 teaspoon baking powder
¼ teaspoon salt
½ cup mulberry juice
Lemon Glaze (See next page)

1. Preheat oven to 350°F (175°C). Generously grease 1 10-inch springform tube pan.
2. Heat shortening, syrup and sugar in a large saucepan over medium heat until sugar melts. Remove from heat.
3. Add dairy sour cream, beaten eggs and mulberries. Set aside.
4. In a small bowl, sift together dry ingredients and add to saucepan to make batter. Mix well and pour into prepared springform pan. Bake 30 minutes, or until knife inserted comes out dry.
5. Pour mulberry juice over cooled cake to moisten. Top with Lemon Glaze.

Makes 20 servings.

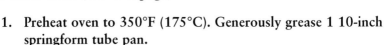

Lemon Glaze

1 tablespoon milk
2 tablespoons lemon juice
¾ cup confectioner's sugar

In a small bowl, gradually blend milk and lemon juice into
confectioners' sugar. Dribble over cake.

Enough for 1 cake.

Cream Cheese Frosting

This never-fail frosting is easy to make. I sometimes add lemon or lime
juice to give it a little tang.

1 pound confectioner's sugar
2 teaspoons vanilla extract
1 8-ounce package cream cheese, softened
1 cup butter, softened
½ cup chopped pecans
¼ cup shredded coconut
Dash of salt

1. In a medium-size bowl, thoroughly combine all ingredients
   except pecans and coconut.
2. Frost cake and decorate top with pecans and coconut.

Yields frosting for 2 8-inch layers, top and sides.

New Mexico's first pecan trees were planted in the early 1900s at the
New Mexico State University horticulture farm by Fabian Garcia.
More trees were planted across the Mesilla Valley in following years,
and the first commercial orchard was established by Dean Stahmann,
Sr., south of Las Cruces in the 1930s. By 1970, close to 9,000 acres of
pecan orchards were established, and more pecan trees were being
planted. New Mexico now produces approximately 20% of the U.S.
pecan crop each year and, in 2006, became the largest pecan
producing state in the nation. The area around Roswell where I live
has large pecan orchards.

Mexican Wedding Cakes

Similar to a shortbread cookie, these melt-in-your-mouth little cakes are popular here at weddings, Christmas, christenings and many other special occasions. Be sure to use the best quality butter and pure vanilla extract to make these festive taste treats.

2 sticks of butter at room temperature
2 teaspoons pure vanilla extract
2 cups all purpose flour
1 cup pecans, toasted and coarsely ground
2 cups powdered sugar, divided
⅛ teaspoon ground cinnamon, divided

1. Preheat oven to 350°F (175°C).
2. In a large bowl, beat butter using an electric mixer until light and fluffy.
3. Beat in the flour, then pecans.
4. Divide dough in half and form each half into a ball. Wrap each ball in plastic and chill in refrigerator until cold, about 30 minutes.
5. In a pie dish, whisk ½ of the powdered sugar and cinnamon and blend. Set aside.
6. Working with ½ of the dough, roll about 2 teaspoons of the dough between the palms of your hands to make a ball. Repeat until all of the first half of the dough is used. Arrange balls on heavy large prepared baking sheet, spaced about 2 inches apart.
7. Place baking sheet in oven and bake until golden brown on top, about 18 minutes.
8. Remove from oven and, while still hot, toss in pie dish to coat completely. Transfer warm cookies to rack and allow to cool.
9. Repeat procedure with remaining half of dough.
10. Sift remaining powdered sugar and cinnamon over cool cookies and serve.

Depending on size of dough balls, makes 36 to 40 little cakes.

Natillas

This custard is similar to flan but is typically richer, makes a generous use of cinnamon flavoring and does not use caramel. Light and smooth, this traditional dessert is very common here in New Mexico households.

4 eggs, separated
¾ cup sugar
one-quarter cup all-purpose flour
⅛ teaspoon salt
4 cups milk
½ teaspoon vanilla extract
ground cinnamon

1. In a medium-size bowl, beat egg yolks; stir in sugar, flour and salt. Thoroughly combine. Add 2 tablespoons of milk and mix.
2. In a saucepan, scald remaining milk (heat just until bubbles begin to form around the outside)
3. Stirring constantly, add egg yolks and sugar/flour mixture. Reduce heat and simmer until mixture is the consistency of a thick custard.
4. Remove from heat and allow to cool; stir in the vanilla extract.
5. In a large bowl, beat egg whites until they are stiff. Fold custard mixture into beaten egg whites.
6. Sprinkle with the ground cinnamon and set aside for 30 minutes. Serve warm or chilled.

Makes 4 servings.

Pecan Pie

One of the wonderful desserts introduced to New Mexico after the Civil War, when many Southern troops came west and brought pecans with them.

1 cup all-purpose unbleached flour
¼ teaspoon salt
⅓ cup shortening
2 tablespoons cold water
¼ cup sugar
2 tablespoons all-purpose flour
½ teaspoon salt
1 cup dark corn syrup
2 eggs, lightly beaten
½ cup evaporated milk
1 teaspoon vanilla extract
1 cup pecans

1. To make crust, mix flour and salt; using a pastry blender or 2 knives, cut in shortening until the mixture resembles course meal. Gently toss with a fork, adding enough water to barely hold together. Remove from mixing bowl form into a ball. Wrap in plastic and refrigerate at least 20 minutes.
2. Preheat oven to 375°F (190°C). On a lightly floured surface, roll dough into a 10-inch circle. Patting gently, fit into a 9-inch pie pan. Fold dough under the lip of pie plate to form an edge; using your fingers, flute the top of the edge. Prick the dough with fork; refrigerate while making the filling.
3. To make the filling, mix sugar, flour and salt. Mix in corn syrup. Add eggs, milk and vanilla; stir until smooth. Stir in pecans. Pour filling into the piecrust and bake in the center of the oven for 45-50 minutes. About 20 minutes into the cooking, you may want to use a piecrust protector, or tent the edges of the piecrust with aluminum foil the prevent the piecrust edges from burning. Cool to room temperature before serving.

Makes 8 servings.

Pineapple Cake

I recently went to a party and was served a piece of cake that brought back memories of my youth. The lady who brought the cake was Kana Laymon from Ruidoso, New Mexico. She gave me the recipe and called it "Mexican Wedding Cake." I realized it was the same cake my Aunt Tiny used to bake in the 1940s, calling it her "Pineapple Cake." When I checked our old family recipe file, it was indeed the same recipe. Easy to prepare, it's one you should try for a change in pace.

2 cups all-purpose flour
2 cups white sugar
2 teaspoons baking soda
2 eggs, beaten
1 teaspoon vanilla extract
1 20-ounce can crushed pineapple with juice
½ cup pecans, chopped
frosting:
1 8-ounce package cream cheese
½ cup butter, at room temperature
1½ cups confectioners sugar
1 teaspoon vanilla extract

1. Preheat oven to 350°F (175° C).
2. In a large bowl, mix together the flour, sugar and baking soda. Make a well in the center and add the eggs, vanilla, crushed pineapple with liquid from can and nuts. Mix to blend.
3. Pour into a 9 x 13-inch greased and floured pan. Bake for 45 minutes or until a toothpick inserted into the center comes out clean.
4. To make frosting: in a medium bowl, combine cream cheese, butter, confectioners sugar and vanilla extract. Beat until creamy. Spread evenly on cake.

Serves 8.

Pumpkin Loaf

Pumpkins were another gift that Native Americans shared with the Spanish who came to New Mexico. Here is one the best uses of pumpkin I know of (except of course, Pumpkin-Pecan Cake on the next page).

1 cup packed brown sugar
½ cup granulated sugar
1 cup cooked or canned pumpkin
½ cup vegetable oil
2 eggs
2 cups all-purpose flour
1 teaspoon baking soda
½ teaspoon grated nutmeg
½ teaspoon cinnamon
¼ teaspoons ground ginger
1 cup raisins
½ cup chopped pecans
¼ cup water

1. Preheat oven to 350°F (175°C); grease and flour a 9 x 5-inch pan.
2. Place sugars, pumpkin, oil and eggs in a large bowl; beat well. Sift flour, baking soda, nutmeg, cinnamon and ginger; stir into pumpkin mixture. Add raisins, pecans and water; mix well.
3. Spoon into prepared pan and bake 1¼ to 1½ hours or until done. Cool on wire rack.
4. Let stand uncovered overnight and then slice. Cake is better after 24 hours rest.

Makes 8 servings.

Pumpkin Pecan Cake

Young, tender succulent pumpkin's mild sweet flavor is perfect for baking. Ever year I find more new ways to utilize this wonderful member of the gourd family.

½ cup shortening
1½ cups sugar
3 eggs
1 cup cooked or canned pumpkin
⅔ cup milk
1¾ cups all-purpose flour
½ cup dry powdered milk
2 teaspoons baking powder
1 teaspoon baking soda
1 teaspoon salt
2 teaspoons ground cinnamon
¼ teaspoon ground allspice
½ teaspoon grated nutmeg
¼ teaspoon ground ginger
1 cup coarsely chopped pecans
Lemon Glaze (See page 165)

1. Preheat oven to 350°F (175°C). Lightly grease and flour a 13 x 9-inch pan. In a large bowl, cream shortening and sugar until fluffy. Beat eggs in one at a time.
2. In a small bowl, combine pumpkin and milk and add to shortening mixture.
3. In a small bowl, sift all dry ingredients together and add the pumpkin mixture.
4. Beat mixture well; add nuts. Turn into prepared pan.
5. Bake about 40 to 50 minutes.
Cool on rack. Frost with Lemon glaze.

Makes 10 to 12 servings.

Spanish Fritters

These fluted fritters are common in New Mexico households. Sometimes called Mexican donuts, this is my personal favorite of the Latin treats.

1 cup sugar
2 teaspoons ground cinnamon
1 cup water
2 tablespoons butter
2 tablespoons vegetable shortening
1 tablespoon sugar
½ teaspoon salt
½ cup white cornmeal
½ cup all-purpose flour
2 large eggs
oil for frying

1. In a small dish, combine sugar and cinnamon; set aside. In a 3-quart saucepan, bring water, butter, shortening, sugar and salt to a full boil.
2. Remove from heat and briskly stir in cornmeal and flour.
3. Reduce heat to low; return pan to heat and stir vigorously until ball of dough is formed.
4. Remove from heat and immediately place dough in food processor. Add eggs. Process about 20 seconds, until smooth and shiny.
5. Heat 3 inches of oil in a deep, heavy skillet or deep fryer to 375°F (190°C).
6. Transfer dough to a pastry bag fitted with #5 Star tip. Pipe 8 to 10-inch strips of dough into hot oil. Fry on both sides until browned and crisp, being careful to keep oil a constant 375°F (190°C) for even cooking.
7. Drain on paper towels; roll in sugar and cinnamon mixture to coat.

Makes 8 servings.

Toasted Pecan Coconut Cake

Rich and satisfying, this is a pecan lover's delight. I think this is as good as cake can get, and I don't mind at all using store bought yellow cake mix.

6 tablespoons butter, softened to room temperature
1 cup finely-chopped pecans
2 cups shredded sweetened coconut
1 yellow cake mix (18.25-ounce) plus required ingredients specified on package
1 8-ounce package cream cheese, softened
2 teaspoons milk
3 cups confectioners' sugar
1 teaspoon vanilla extract

1. Preheat oven according to directions on cake mix box. Generously grease 3 8-inch baking pans.
2. Melt 3 tablespoons butter in a skillet over medium heat.
3. Add pecans and coconut to skillet and stir until mixture is golden brown. Remove from skillet and drain on paper towels.
4. Mix cake according to directions on box. Add 1 cup of toasted pecan-coconut mixture. Divide batter among prepared pans and bake as directed on the box. Remove from oven and cool.
5. To make frosting, in a medium bowl, cream remaining butter with cream cheese until light and fluffy. Stir in milk and vanilla extract. Add sugar one cup at a time, beating well until mixture reaches spreading consistency.
6. Reserve ½ cup toasted mixture to spread on top. Add remaining mixture to frosting. Frost cake and sprinkle with reserved toasted mixture.

Makes 10 servings.

Zucchini Pineapple Cake

Just as you thought you knew every way to use zucchini, here it joins pineapple for a great ending to hot, spicy New Mexican meal.

3 eggs
2 cups sugar
2 tablespoons vanilla extract
1 cup oil
2 cups peeled and grated zucchini
3 cups all-purpose flour
1 teaspoon baking powder
1 teaspoon salt
1 teaspoon baking soda
1 teaspoon ground cinnamon
1 cup chopped pecans
1 cup crushed pineapple, drained
Cream Cheese Frosting (See page 165)

1. Preheat oven to 325°F (160°C). Generously grease 2 8-inch cake pans.
2. In a large bowl, beat eggs until fluffy; add sugar, vanilla extract, oil and zucchini; mix well.
3. In a medium-size bowl, mix dry ingredients and stir into egg mixture. Add pecans and pineapple.
4. Pour batter into prepared pans and bake 1 hour. Allow to cool.
5. Frost cooled cake with Cream Cheese Frosting.

Makes 10 servings.

COOKIES & CANDIES

No New Mexico cookbook would be complete without including a selection of the delectable cookies and candies unique to the area. I have picked out some of my personal favorites as well as some old standards. These will tempt even those without a sweet tooth!

I think my wife's Pecan Fudge is as good as fudge gets. The holidays would not be the same in our household without it. Rich, creamy and easy to make, this is one you should try.

No New Mexico Christmas is complete without Biscochitos. The biscochito is the official state cookie of New Mexico. Halfway between a shortbread and a sugar cookie, they are often baked in fancy shapes and are enjoyed by young and old alike.

I've also included one of my oldest recipes, one for Bunkhouse Cookies. This stick-to-your-ribs-cookie was carried horseback by cowboys and was regular fare on cattle ranches here in New Mexico. I was raised on these hearty old-style cookies. Although I use pecans in most of my cookies, many times I'll use Valencia peanuts, which are also grown here.

Biscochitos

Each year when the Christmas holidays approach, out come the Biscochitos, and I have to watch myself or I gain five pounds. As with any traditional food, many recipes exist for these cookies. Here's one I like.

6 cups unbleached all-purpose flour
1 teaspoon baking powder
1 teaspoon salt
1 pound butter, softened
1½ cups sugar
2 teaspoons anise seeds
2 eggs
½ cup brandy

Topping
⅓ cup sugar
3 teaspoons ground cinnamon

1. Preheat oven to 350°F (175°C).
2. In a large bowl. Combine flour with baking powder and salt.
3. In another bowl, cream butter and sugar. Add anise seeds; beat until light.
4. In another bowl, beat eggs at high speed for 2 minutes. Combine eggs and butter mixture.
5. Add flour mixture, 1 cup at a time, mixing well after each addition.
6. Pour brandy over the dough and mix well.
7. On a lightly floured surface, roll dough to ¼ inch thick; cut into desired shapes. In a small bowl, combine sugar and cinnamon. Dip each cookie in sugar and cinnamon topping mix; place on an ungreased baking sheet. Bake in preheated oven 10 to 12 minutes until golden brown. Remove from oven. Sprinkle with additional sugar and cinnamon topping mix.

Makes 72 small cookies.

Bunkhouse Cookies

Here is a rich and hearty old standard from my homestead background.

1 cup butter or shortening
¾ cup packed brown sugar
¾ cup granulated sugar
2 eggs
1¼ cups all-purpose flour
2 cups regular (not quick) uncooked oats
1 teaspoon ground cinnamon
1 teaspoon baking soda
½ teaspoon salt, optional

Topping
1 teaspoon sugar
1 teaspoon ground cinnamon

1. Preheat oven to 375°F (190°C). Grease a baking sheet.
2. In a large bowl, beat together butter, brown sugar, and granulated sugar until light and fluffy.
3. Add eggs and mix well.
4. In a medium-size bowl, combine flour, oats, cinnamon, baking soda and salt. Add to sugar mixture and mix well.
5. Drop by rounded teaspoonful onto prepared baking sheet. Bake 8 to 10 minutes. Cool 1 minute before removing to cooling rack.
6. In a small bowl, combine sugar and cinnamon for topping; sprinkle lightly over each cookie.

Makes about 60 to 70 cookies.

Bunuelos

Served at a number of festive occasions, these fried breads are not the same as the Sopapillas or Indian Fry Bread, two other New Mexico treats. There are many different recipes for these treats, but this is my favorite. They're well worth the effort it takes to make them.

½ cup warm water (105 to 110°F)
2 tablespoons white sugar
2 packages active dry yeast
1 cup milk
4 level tablespoons shortening
½ teaspoon salt
2 cups unbleached all-purpose flour
vegetable oil for frying
topping:
½ cup white sugar
1 teaspoon cinnamon

1. In a small bowl, mix together warm water and sugar. Sprinkle yeast over mixture and let set for 10 to 12 minutes. You should then see froth forming on top and be able to smell the yeast.
2. In a small saucepan, heat milk over medium heat. Add shortening and salt. Remove from heat as soon as shortening melts and bubbles appear around the edge (do not boil). Cool mixture to lukewarm. If it is too hot, it will destroy the action of the yeast and the dough will not rise.
3. Sift flour into a large mixing bowl. Stir in yeast and milk mixtures then stir briskly to fully combine. When mixture becomes too thick to mix with a spoon, turn out onto a lightly floured surface and knead for at least 5 minutes. The dough should smooth, elastic and not too sticky. It should spring back when you poke your finger into it. Form into a ball.
4. In a large bowl, place a small amount of vegetable oil. Roll the dough ball in the oil until it is evenly coated. Cover bowl with plastic wrap. Allow the dough to rise in a warm place until it

doubles in size. Depending on temperature, this should take about 1 or 2 hours.

5. When dough has risen, punch it down, cut it into 4 equal sections and allow it to rest for an additional 10 minutes.

6. Divide each dough quarter into 6 or 8 equal pieces. Pat each piece into a circular shape and then stretch and press until a round shape is formed.

7. While dough shapes are resting, in a skillet or electric fryer, heat oil to 375°F (175°C).

8. Carefully place dough pieces into hot oil until they puff up and brown, approximately 1 minute. With a slotted spoon, flip over and cook an additional minute to brown second side. Remove from oil and drain well.

9. Place sugar and cinnamon in a large paper bag and mix thoroughly. Place 2 or 3 warm bunuelos in bag and shake to coat.

Serves 6 or 8.

Empanaditas

For this type of recipe, I find the use of frozen puff pastry from the supermarket's frozen food department to be a great time-saver. I used pumpkin for this recipe, but you can use fresh or canned fruits to make these little stuffed pies.

1 package of frozen puff pastry
1 cup canned pumpkin
1 cup firmly packed brown sugar
1 tablespoon unsalted butter
1 teaspoon ground cinnamon
1 teaspoon pumpkin pie spice
¼ cup chopped pecans
Topping:
1 egg
1 teaspoon water
coarse or white decorator sugar

1. Set out puff pastry about 20 to 30 minutes before ready to use.
2. Roll out pastry to ⅛-inch thickness. Cut with 3 inch round cookie cutter to make dough circles. Set aside.
3. In a saucepan, combine pumpkin, brown sugar, butter, cinnamon, pumpkin pie spice and pecans. Cook over medium heat, stirring constantly until mixture is thickened. Cool completely (45–60 minutes).
4. Preheat oven to 400°F (205°C).
5. Place a rounded teaspoon of pumpkin mixture in center of each dough circle. Fold one side of each circle over the other to from a crescent shaped empanaditas. Pinch together and press edges together with a fork lightly to seal. Place on an ungreased cookie sheet.
6. Whisk together egg and water in a small bowl. Brush egg mixture lightly over tops of empanaditas. Sprinkle with sugar. Bake 12 to 15 minutes or until lightly browned.

Makes about 24.

Honey-Nut Cookies

Once you try these easy-to-make cookies, you will understand why I love them

1 cup butter
1 cup honey
1 cup sugar
1 egg
3 cups all-purpose flour
2 teaspoons baking powder
2 teaspoons ground ginger
½ teaspoon vanilla extract
1½ cups coarsely chopped pecans or peanuts

1. Preheat oven to 375°F (190°C). Grease baking sheet and, because you are using honey, preheat the sheet just before adding the cookie dough.
2. In a large-size bowl, cream butter; beat in honey, sugar and egg.
3. Stir in flour, baking powder and ground ginger; mix thoroughly. Stir in vanilla extract and nuts.
4. Drop by teaspoon onto preheated baking sheets and bake about 10 to 12 minutes.

Makes about 70 cookies.

Mexican Wedding Cookies

These cookies are traditionally served at New Mexico weddings. There are a number of secrets to making these cookies, among them the use of high quality butter and pure vanilla extract.

¾ cup pecans
2 cups all-purpose flour
½ cup confections' sugar
1 cup butter, slightly softened
1 teaspoon pure vanilla extract
½ teaspoon almond extract

Toppings:
1 cup confectioners' sugar

1. Place pecans in food processor with 1 cup of the flour. Using a pulsing method, grind together until nuts are fine.
2. In a medium-size bowl, beat sugar with butter. If butter is too soft, the cookie dough will be difficult to work. Stir in vanilla and almond extracts.
3. Add nut-flour mixture to the butter. Beat in remaining cup flour. Refrigerate dough 20 minutes.
4. Preheat oven to 350°F (175°C).
5. Shape dough into walnut-sized balls and place on ungreased baking sheets.
6. Bake in preheated oven 10 to 12 minutes. Remove cookies to a cooling rack.
7. When cookies have cooled about 15 minutes, roll in confectioners' sugar until completely coated.

Makes about 30 cookies.

Millie's Pecan Fudge

My wife, Millie, has made this soft, creamy fudge for as long as I can remember. The holidays would not be the same without her wonderful fudge.

4½ cups sugar
1 cup evaporated milk
15 ounces of plain Hershey candy bars, broken into small pieces
1 12-ounce package semi-sweet chocolate chips
1 7-ounce jar marshmallow creme
1½ teaspoons salt
1 teaspoon vanilla extract
2 cups chopped pecans
¼ cup butter

1. Combine sugar and evaporated milk in a heavy 2½ quart saucepan. Over medium heat, bring to a full boil, stirring constantly.
2. Continue boiling 5 minutes over medium heat, or until candy thermometer reaches 234°F (110°C), stirring constantly.
3. In large-size mixing bowl, place Hershey candy pieces, chocolate chips, marshmallow creme, salt and vanilla extract.
4. Pour hot sugar mixture over chocolate, one half at a time. Mix thoroughly after each pour.
5. Add pecans and butter and mix well.

Makes about 36 pieces.

Roswell Fours

For decades these caramels were made by a women's group for an annual fund-raiser at the Roswell Episcopal church. Although the ladies finally stopped making them in the 90s, these wonderful treats are almost as famous as the UFOS that Roswell is known for. I have made a couple minor changes to the original recipe to update it, and I hope you will try it. Hint: be sure not to attempt to make them on a cloudy, wet day.

1 cup packed dark brown sugar
1 cup dark corn syrup
2 sticks unsalted butter, cut into chunks
⅛ teaspoon salt
2 cups half-and-half or heavy cream
1 tablespoon pure vanilla extract, combined with 1 tablespoon hot water
1½ cups toasted pecans , chopped
1 pound unsweetened chocolate of choice (l like the dark type)

1. Line a 9 x 13 inch-baking dish with aluminum foil, leave a little extra over 2 sides. Coat foil with cooking spray.
2. In a heavy, non-reactive 6-quart pot, thoroughly stir together the brown sugar, corn syrup, butter and salt. Stir in the half and half. When the sugar dissolves, bring to a boil over medium-high heat, stirring constantly with a wooden spoon.
3. Adjust the heat so the mixture boils briskly. Insert candy thermometer. Continue boiling briskly, occasionally gently stirring and scraping the pot bottom, until the mixture thickens and darkens somewhat, 8 to 9 minutes.
4. Reduce the heat and continue boiling, gently stirring and scraping to avoid scorching, until the caramel reaches 244°F (soft ball stage).
5. Immediately remove from heat. Gently stir in the vanilla and water mixture and nuts, until evenly distributed.

6. Pour the caramel into the baking dish. Cool at least 1½ hours, then invert dish on a board. Lift dish from caramel and cut into 1-inch squares.
7. In a glass dish, heat chocolate in microwave until melted and then dip caramels. Set aside on wax paper to cool.

Makes approximately 50 caramels.

Pecan Drops

This is an elegant way to use pecan halves. I sometimes use mint chocolate chips and roasted pecans.

1 cup firmly packed brown sugar
⅓ cup evaporated milk
2 tablespoons corn syrup
6 ounces semi-sweet chocolate chips
½ cup chopped pecans
1 teaspoon vanilla extract
36 pecan halves.

1. Combine brown sugar, evaporated milk and corn syrup in a heavy saucepan.
2. Bring to a boil over medium heat, stirring constantly, and boil 2 minutes. Remove from heat. Add chocolate chips, chopped pecans and vanilla extract; stir until chocolate is melted and mixture is slightly thickened.
3. Drop by rounded teaspoons onto waxed-paper-lined baking sheets. Press pecan halves on top. Chill until firm, about 30 minutes.

Makes approximately 36 candies.

Piñon Brittle

I sometimes add the piñon nuts with the vanilla and soda, after the syrup has reached the hard-crack stage; it's a matter of choice.

2 teaspoons butter, for coating baking sheets
2 cups sugar
1 cup white corn syrup
½ cup water
1 tablespoon butter
2 cups raw piñon nuts
1 teaspoon vanilla extract
2 teaspoons baking powder

1. Using 2 teaspoons of butter, coat one large or two small baking sheets.
2. In a large-size saucepan, combine sugar, corn syrup and water. Cook, stirring occasionally, until mixture reaches 234°F (110°C) on a candy thermometer or forms a soft ball when drizzled into ice water.
3. Add the tablespoon of butter and the nuts; continue cooking and stirring until it reaches 300°F (150°C) or hardens and cracks when drizzled into ice water.
4. Quickly remove form heat. Add vanilla extract and soda; mix well. Immediately pour as thinly as possible onto prepared sheets.

Makes 6 servings.

The piñon nut comes from the piñon (Pinus edulis) tree, the official state tree of New Mexico. These small nuts are very tasty, and, in a good year, you will find them available from sellers by the side of the road all over the northern part of the state. Because they are totally dependent on rainfall, they are not always available. As many as 4 millon pounds are harvested in a good year here in New Mexico.

APPENDIX

GLOSSARY

Anasazi Beans
One of the most popular of the modern boutique beans, the Anasazi bean is also called the Aztec bean, Cave bean, New Mexico Appaloosa and sometimes Jacob's Cattle. This attractive purple-red and white bean cooks in about ⅔ the time of an ordinary pinto bean to a creamy, even pink color. It has a sweet mild full flavor and a mealy texture, perfect for any New Mexico recipe.

Ancho Chiles
Ancho chiles are ripened and dried poblano chiles. These are the most popular dried chiles in Mexico. They vary from sweet to moderate heat.

Anise Seeds
Sweet and aromatic, these small elongated seeds taste like licorice. Anise seeds are used whole or crushed in a variety of foods including baked goods, stews, cheese, pickles, fish and shellfish.

Avocado
Although many believe the avocado to be a vegetable, it is actually a fruit. It has a leathery skin and a soft, buttery flesh that yields to light pressure when ripe. Hard avocados will ripen if left on the counter for a few days. Haas avocados (California type) are smaller and darker than the emerald colored fruits grown in Florida. To keep avocados from discoloring after peeling, brush or sprinkle them with lemon juice. Even then, they should be peeled as close to serving time as possible.

Beans, Dried
A western staple, dried beans keep almost indefinitely. Before cooking, rinse beans well and sort through them, tossing out any small stones or other matter. Some beans require soaking prior to cooking. Cook beans slowly on the stove top, in a crockpot or in a

pressure cooker. Cooking times vary depending on the variety of bean. Properly prepared, cooked beans are tender but still firm. When you are short of time or only need a small amount of beans, you will find canned varieties useful, although they are sometimes mushy.

Bell Peppers

Bell peppers are the only member of the genus *capsicum* to lack capsaicin; hence they lack the hotness of taste and are comparatively "sweet." They can be green, red, yellow, orange and, more rarely. white, purple and brown. Until recently, bell peppers of any color other than green were rarely available. The green pepper is actually an immature red pepper. Bell peppers become sweeter as they ripen, with the green slightly bitter and the red and yellow the sweetest. Bell peppers, particularly the red ones, are an excellent source of both vitamin C and beta carotene.

Big Jim Chiles

Big Jim chiles are available in mild, medium hot and hot varieties and are the most commonly available fresh (and freshly roasted) chiles in New Mexico and the Southwest.

Black Beans (**frijoles negros,** turtle beans)

These small dark beans have a hearty flavor. They are often used in South American cooking, and their very dark purple-blue color makes them attractive in salsas.

Black Pepper

Peppercorns (*piper nigrum*) came to the Western world originally from Madagascar. The success of medieval spice traders made black pepper more widely available, and now ground pepper is one of the most common spices in European and American cuisine; it is found on nearly every dinner table in many parts of the world. Pepper looses its potency quickly after being ground; for best results, buy peppercorns and a small pepper mill, grinding only what you need.

Black-Eyed Peas (cowpeas)

These are the seeds of the cowpea, an annual vine. Their tan coloring with black spots gives them the name "black-eyed." According to legend, black-eyed peas are supposed to provide good luck when consumed on New Years Day.

Cascabel Chiles

Fresh cascabel chiles are round, about 1-1/2 inches in diameter. They are quite hot and have a distinctive flavor; drying them gives them a nutty taste.

Cayenne Pepper, cayenne chiles

Cayenne chiles are extremely hot, small, narrow red peppers. Ground red pepper is made from ground dried cayenne chiles and is often called cayenne pepper. The name originally came from the city of Cayenne, in French Guiana. Cayenne is usually used in its ground form, although some types of cooking (for example, Szechuan) do use whole chiles. Cayenne also has been used for centuries for its medicinal properties, most notably for gastrointestinal and circulatory problems.

Cheddar Cheese

Cheddar cheese is a firm cheese made from cow's milk. It originated in the English village of Cheddar in Somerset and becomes sharper with age. Cheddar cheese is available in several varieties, including mild, medium, sharp, New York Style, Longhorn, white and Vermont. In recipes calling for Cheddar cheese, you can use any variety and will probably get the best results using the one you prefer.

Cheese

Cheese is nutritious dairy food made from the milk of cows, sheep, goats and other mammals. There are hundreds of types of cheese produced all over the world. Cheddar and Monterey Jack are the most commonly used cheeses in Southwestern cooking.

Chevre Cheese

Chevre cheese is pure white goat cheese. With a delightfully tart flavor that easily distinguishes it from other cheeses, chevre cheese can range in texture from moist and creamy to dry and semi-firm. It comes in a variety of shapes and takes on a sour taste when it is old. After opening, always wrap it tightly and store in refrigerator.

Chickpeas
See garbanzo beans.

Chile Peppers
Chile peppers are vegetables of the pod-bearing *capsicum* family. There are hundreds of varieties of chiles, and new strains are being developed frequently. Whether whole, dry, crushed or powdered, they are the heart and soul of New Mexico cuisine. Fresh, they are considered a vegetable, not just a spice. Fresh chile is seasonally available, but frozen, canned and dried are available year round.

Chile Powder
Pure chile powder is made from finely ground dried chiles. It is usually made from red chiles and comes in a variety of flavors and heat levels.

Chili Powder
Chili powder is a spice mix usually consisting of chile powder and other spices and herbs, including cumin, garlic and oregano.

Chipotle Chiles
Chipotle chiles are smoked and dried jalapeños with a very wrinkly brown appearance. They have a unique smoky taste and are very hot.

Chocolate
The first use of chocolate has been credited to the Mayan and Aztec cultures, who used the beans of the cocoa (*cacao*) tree as a form of currency and as a bitter ceremonial drink after the beans were crushed into a paste. Spanish explorers brought some back to Europe from the New World, and eventually its use spread, at first only for the elite who could afford it. The Europeans sweetened the chocolate with sugar and its popularity grew. Eventually the Industrial Revolution made it readily available to everyone. European and American chocolate is sweetened with sugar, while Mexican chocolate frequently contains cinnamon, vanilla, cloves and ground almonds as well as sugar.

Chorizo

Chorizo is a spicy, highly flavorful sausage usually made from pork (or pork and beef), chile, garlic and other spices. It is available both in links and in bulk and is most commonly used with eggs and other breakfast recipes.

Cilantro

Cilantro (Mexican parsley, Chinese parsley, fresh coriander) is actually the name for the leaves of the coriander plant. These leaves are similar in appearance to flat-leaf parsley but have a completely different flavor, with a citrusy biting tang that people seem to either love or hate. Cilantro adds its distinctive flavor to many dishes and is often used as a garnish. To keep it fresh, store it in the refrigerator with the stems in water and plastic loosely covering the leafy tops.

Cinnamon

Cinnamon is a spice derived from the bark of the cinnamon tree, a small evergreen originally native to southern India and Ceylon (Sri Lanka). It is sold in sticks (actually tightly wound quills) or ground as a powder. In addition to all kinds of dishes from sweet-savory to sweet, cinnamon is used for medicinal purposes, and cinnamon oil is even used as an insecticide.

Coriander

Coriander is an annual herb of the parsley family. Its leaves are referred to as cilantro. As a spice, the word "coriander" refers to the seeds (or small fruits), which have a dusky citrus flavor and are often associated in Eastern cooking. Coriander can be purchased ground or as whole dried seeds.

Cornhusks

When corn is harvested, the husks are removed and dried. In food preparation, all silk is removed from the husks, which are then softened by soaking and are used to wrap food before it is cooked, making a natural jacket to hold food together while steaming. Several small cornhusks may be overlapped to make larger wrappings, as in tamale preparation.

Cornmeal

Cornmeal is a staple in Southwestern kitchens. It comes coarsely or finely ground in yellow, white and blue. The colors refer to the corn— yellow, white or blue corn. Each type has a slightly different flavor and consistency. Most recipes calling for cornmeal refer to the yellow variety unless specified differently. In general, the white is more delicate while the blue has a stronger flavor and tougher texture.

Cottage Cheese

Cottage cheese is made from separating milk or cream into curds and whey. The result is a soft, spoonable cheese that is white and mild but faintly sour in taste. It is often made from low-fat or skim milk.

Cowpeas

See black-eyed peas.

Cream Cheese

Cream cheese is a mildly-tangy, smooth, creamy-textured spreadable cheese. Developed in 1872, this soft cheese is made from cows' milk. Neufchatel cheese can be used in place of cream cheese for a lower butterfat content.

Cumin

Originally cultivated in Persia (Iran) and the Mediterranean region, cumin has been used as an aromatic spice since the days of the Old Testament. This powerful, sometimes dominating spice can be used to season many dishes, as it draws out their natural sweetness. It is traditionally added to Middle-Eastern, Indian, Cuban and Mexican-style foods. It is frequently found in commercially produced chili powder and curry powder. Recipes may call for whole cumin seed or for ground cumin.

Frijoles

See pinto beans.

Garbanzo Beans (chickpeas)

These rounded, beige-colored beans with their nutty flavor and buttery texture are often used in salads. They are also a noted ingredient in many types of Middle Eastern and Indian cuisine such as hummus and falafel.

Habanero Chiles

These lantern-shaped chiles have a fruity flavor and are the hottest of all chiles.

Hominy

Hominy consists of yellow or white corn that has been soaked in lime to remove its germ and hard outer hull, a process dating back 10,000 years in Central American cultures. Now available dried, frozen or canned, hominy is an important ingredient of many popular Mexican and Southwestern recipes, including posole and menudo. In the Southeastern part of the United States, hominy is pressed into patties and fried or ground into small grains called hominy grits.

Jalapeño Chiles

These popular chiles have a good amount of heat—ranging from hot to very hot—and rich flavor. They are about three inches long and usually feature rounded tips—the sharper the tips the hotter the chile. The red ones have a much richer, warmer flavor that the green ones. Try to find fresh jalapeños; canned ones aren't as fiery or as tasty. When smoked and dried they are called chipotle chiles.

Jicama

Also called the Mexican potato or Mexican turnip, the jicama is a brown-skinned root vegetable that looks like a turnip but has a very mild sweet and starchy flavor. To use, remove the peel, including the fibrous flesh directly under the skin. Cut or slice and serve in salads and salsas. You can also sauté it and use it in stir fries; it stays crisp when cooked, similar to water chestnuts. Unlike turnip greens, the leaves of the jicama are inedible.

Juniper Berries

Juniper berries are actually tiny cones of an evergreen shrub, the juniper. These blue-green berries are used in northern European and Scandinavian cooking to enhance the flavor of meats and wild game; they also give gin its distinctive flavor. In herbal medicine, they have a variety of medicinal purposes including treating urinary tract infections.

Lard

Lard is a soft white solid or semi-solid animal fat produced from rendered pig fat. UpigError! Bookmark not defined.. Until recent years when it was deemed to be unhealthy compared to vegetable fats, lard was one of the most frequently used ingredients in traditional New Mexican cooking. Certain items such as pie crusts, tortillas, sopaillas and biscochitos simply do not have the traditional taste or texture when another fat is substituted for lard. Because of its reputation, freshly rendered lard is rarely available and the processed flavorless blocks in your supermarket are of little value. I have used vegetable oil in most recipes. If you have fresh lard available, by all means use it. There is no substitute for the taste it offers. It should be noted that lard, for all its reputation, has approximately half the cholesterol of butter and no trans fat.

Mango

Once known as the "food of the Gods" in Southern and Southeast Asia, the mango is one of the most popular fruits in Mexico and growing in popularity in New Mexico. It has a very sweet peach-like taste and flowery aroma. The flesh is juicy and deep yellow. To slice the fruit, free it from the pit in large pieces. The large fruit trees grow in tropical and subtropical climates throughout the world. It is especially delicious in salsa.

Masa

Masa literally means "dough" in Spanish, although it is generally understood to mean "corn dough." It is made from dried corn kernels that have been softened in a lime (calcium hydroxide) solution, then ground. Fresh frozen masa is sometimes available in your supermarket. Masa harina is dried, powdered masa. It is readily available and can be used in any recipe that calls for masa.

Mole

Mole is the Spanish word for "mixture" or "concoction." Dozens of different mole sauces, quite unlike each other, are used in contemporary Mexico. In New Mexico, the mole sauce usually indicated is the one with the more complete name "mole poblano." This dark brown sauce is created with a mixture of dried chile peppers (usually ancho, pasillo, mulatto, poblano and/or chipotle), nuts, spices, various other ingredients and unsweetened chocolate, which gives the sauce its unique taste. Incidentally, the final "e" is pronounced, unlike in the name of the digging animal, the mole.

Monterey Jack Cheese

Made from cow's milk and developed by Franciscan monks in Monterey, California, Monterey Jack cheese has a buttery, bland taste and melts easily, making it a favorite for hot sandwiches and various recipes. An aged version of this cheese, known as Dry Jack, is harder and can be grated.

Mozzarella Cheese

Mozzarella cheese is a white cheese made from either whole or partially skimmed cow's milk. It has a firm texture and is usually available in sliced, small round or shredded form. The "low moisture" varieties may have preservatives added.

New Mexico 6 (formerly Anaheim) Chiles

The mildest variety of chile, these taste pretty much like bell peppers with a bit of a bite.

New Mexico Chiles

New Mexico chiles are relatively slim and range in length from five to eight inches and in color from light green to deep red. There are two main varieties of New Mexico chiles—New Mexico 6 (formerly Anaheim) and Big Jim—which vary from mild to hot.

Nonreactive Cookware

Certain metals, especially aluminum, react with the acids in chiles and tomatoes. These acids can actually leach the metal away and into the foods and can affect color and flavor as well. Do not store processed chiles or tomatoes in aluminum containers. Uncoated copper and cast iron cookware are also reactive. Nonreactive cookware is made from clay, coated copper (unscratched), enamel, glass, plastic or stainless steel. Aluminum pans with a Teflon or other protective coating are considered nonreactive as long as they are not scratched.

Nuts
Nuts are important flavoring agents in Southwestern cooking and are sometimes ground and stirred into sauces as a thickening agent, adding flavor and body. Toasted nuts are often used as a garnish or in baking. Pecans, peanuts and piñon (pine) nuts are popular nuts in New Mexico.

Nuts, Ground
Ground nuts are often called for in Southwestern recipes. To grind nuts, place 1/3 to 1/2 cup at a time in the work bowl of a food processor or blender. Process them in short pulses just until ground. Too much grinding will give you nut butter.

Nuts, Toasted
Toasting nuts enhances their flavor. To toast nuts, spread them in a single layer on an ungreased pan or cookie sheet; bake at 350°F (175°C), stirring occasionally until they are done. Nuts are toasted when they are lightly browned. Almonds, pecans and walnuts take 7 to 12 minutes. Pine nuts toast more rapidly, in 5 to 7 minutes.

Papaya
The papaya is a nearly oval fruit with a creamy golden yellow skin, orange-yellow flesh and scores of shiny black seeds conveniently packed in its center. The flavor is sweet and somewhat similar to that of a cantaloupe; in some types it tastes quite musky. When slightly underripe, the flesh is firm (perfect for making into relishes and salsas); when ripe, it is soft and very juicy. Rich in vitamin C, the papaya contains the enzyme papain, useful in tenderizing meat and as an ingredient in herbal supplements for digestive and other problems. Originally native to southern Mexico and Central America, the papaya now grows in all tropical and subtropical countries.

Parmesan Cheese

Parmesan cheese is a hard, dry cheese made from skim cow's milk. It has a rich, sharp flavor and is usually graded or shredded for use, particularly in Italian cooking.

Pasilla Chiles

These thin, red-brown chiles have a dusty, raisin-like taste and are of medium heat.

Pecan

The state tree of Texas, the pecan is a species of hickory tree native to the southern United States. Commercial growing of pecans has expanded greatly in Southern New Mexico in recent years. This oil-rich nut has a buttery flavor and is eaten fresh or in salads, desserts and candies.

Pepper

Pepper comes in many forms, all in the genus *capsicum*, including chile, black pepper (peppercorn), bell pepper, cayenne pepper, paprika and pimento. All peppers except the bell pepper include the chemical capsaicin, with makes them hot or bitter to the taste and dissuades mammals from eating them. Capsaicin is also used in medicine as a topical pain reliever for arthritis and other types of pain. See also black pepper, bell peppers and chile peppers.

Picante Sauce

Picante sauce is similar to salsa but usually more pureed. Picante is a Spanish adjective that derives from picar, which means "to sting." The term is often used interchangeably with the term "salsa."

Pico de Gallo

Salsa cruda ("raw sauce"), also known as pico de gallo ("cock's beak"), salsa mexicana ("Mexican sauce") or salsa fresca ("fresh sauce") is made with raw tomatoes, lime juice, chilli peppers, onions, cilantro leaves and other coarsely chopped raw ingredients. It is used as a condiment similar to salsa and is commonly served with tacos and fajitas.

Piñon Nuts

Piñon nuts are the seeds of the piñon (*Pinus edulis*) pine, a two-needled scrubby evergreen that grows wild in New Mexico, Colorado, Arizona and Utah between 5,000 and 8,000 feet in elevation. The piñon is the state tree of New Mexico, and the local Indians have been consuming the nuts for centuries. Raw or toasted, they are delicious by themselves, or they can be enjoyed as an ingredient in or sprinkled on a variety of dishes, salads and desserts. Store them tightly covered in the refrigerator or freezer, depending on how quickly they are to be used.

Pinto Beans (**frijoles**)

These attractive brown-speckled beans have a pale or pinkish background when dry. Cooking changes them to a dull pink or grey-brown. A staple of Southwestern cooking, pinto beans are what you will usually find on your plate in restaurants, whether by the side of enchiladas or wrapped in a burrito.

Poblano Chiles

Poblano chiles are heart shaped, more like a bell pepper, and little darker colored and somewhat sweeter and hotter than the New Mexico Big Jims. They are the chiles most frequently used for chile rellenos.

Pumpkin Seeds

Pumpkin seeds with the shells or husks removed are also known as *pepitas*. These seeds, with their sweet and nutty flavor and a malleable chewy texture, are quite nutritious. Store them in a cool, dry place. To toast pumpkin seeds, spread them in a single layer on an ungreased pan or cookie sheet. Bake at 350°F (175°C) 13 to 15 minutes, stirring and checking frequently. Although they are available year round, they are freshest in the fall when pumpkins are in season.

Queso

Queso is the Spanish word for cheese.

Red Pepper

See cayenne pepper.

Red Pepper Flakes

Red pepper flakes, or crushed red peppers, are just what their name suggests, flaked dried ripe chiles. Most chile flake mixtures are quite hot.

Red Pepper Sauce

Red pepper sauce is a commercially bottled condiment made from vinegar, spices and hot chiles. It adds heat but little in the way of flavor. Many restaurants place small bottles on the table for patrons who want to give their meals a bit of an extra kick. Some cooks keep it on hand for the same reason.

Rice

Rice exists in a large number of varieties, but Mexican cooking usually calls for long- or medium-grain white rice. Other types of rice, such as brown or basmati, may be used, but cooking times will need to be adjusted and the flavor and consistency of the rice will be different. Southwestern dishes sometimes use wild rice, which really isn't rice. It is the seed of an aquatic grass once harvested only by Native Americans who lived by the Great Lakes. and makes a popular side dish, particularly with game.

Ricotta Cheese

This Italian cheese is a by-product from the production of mozzarella and other cheeses. It is similar to cottage cheese in texture, although lighter, sweeter and smoother. Ricotta cheese is a key ingredient in cheesecake and lasagna.

Ristras

Ristras are ropes of dried red chile often used for decoration. Chile pods in ristras can be reconstituted into a red chile puree.

Salsa

A spicy sauce of chopped, usually uncooked fruit and/or vegetables, including tomatoes, onions and chile peppers. Salsa has surpassed ketchup, becoming America's number one condiment.

Salsa Verde

Salsa verde is a cooked Mexican green salsa usually made with tomatillos, hot green peppers, garlic, onion and salt.

Serrano Chiles

Hotter than jalapeños, these chiles are usually shorter and thinner and are a mainstay in salsas.

Squash Blossoms

Squash blossoms from pumpkins are preferred for use in Southwestern cooking because they are larger than those from zucchini, but either can be used. They are extremely perishable and are best used the day they are bought.

Tequila

Tequila is a pale, sharp-tasting liquor distilled from the blue agave plant, which thrives in arid, hot climates like the central plains of Northern Mexico. The liquor is named after the town of Tequila, located in the state of Jalisco, where production started more than 200 years ago. Tequila is a main component of the popular Mexican drink, the margarita. There are many different varieties of tequila and many different types of margaritas.

Tomatillo

Tomatillos are fat little vegetables the size of robust cherry tomatoes. They grow in papery husks reminiscent of Japanese lanterns and taste best when they are brilliant green in color. By the time they begin to turn yellow, they have lost some of their acid freshness. This happens when they are lightly cooked too, but then they develop a gentler flavor and become more luscious. Uncooked, chopped tomatillos are the basis for chunky green salsas. Select tomatillos with their husks still drawn tightly around them. Husk and rinse off the sticky residue before using them.

Tomato

The tomato, a plant native to South America, is widely cultivated for its edible, fleshy, usually red fruit. Roasting tomatoes gives them a faintly mysterious flavor. This works best with truly ripe, red tomatoes. To roast and peel tomatoes, set the oven control to broil. Arrange cored tomatoes with their top surfaces about 5 inches from the heat. Broil, turning occasionally, until the skin is blistered and evenly browned, about 5 to 8 minutes. The skins will be easy to remove. If the tomatoes are roasted on aluminum foil, the cleanup will be easy and you'll be able to save any juice they give off as they roast.

Tortilla

Tortillas are round, flat unleavened breads made from ground wheat or corn. They are the basis of Mexican cookery. Tortillas are rolled, folded, used as dippers, fried crisp and munched fresh. Corn tortillas can be cut into wedges and fried for chips. For the best chips, fry tortillas that are at least one day old. Flour tortillas, softer than those made from corn, are becoming more popular in New Mexico. Commercially made tortillas of both kinds are best stored in the freezer until needed. To soften tortillas, warm them on a hot ungreased skillet or griddle for about 30 seconds to 1 minute. They can also be warmed in a 250°F (120°C) degree oven for 15 minutes. Or, wrap several in dampened microwaveable paper toweling or microwave plastic wrap and microwave on HIGH (100% power) for 15 to 20 seconds. To keep warmed tortillas soft, place in tortilla holder or plastic bag.

Tripe

Tripe usually means the linings of pig and sheep stomachs. Tripe is the identifying ingredient of traditional Menudo, a hearty soup. Tripe needs to be thoroughly rinsed in three or four changes of cold water before it can be used.

Walnuts

Walnuts are a delicious complement to a variety of recipes.

ALTITUDE ADJUSTMENTS

High-altitude baking

If you live at an altitude above 3,000 feet (most of New Mexico), you will find that you may need to make adjustments in many recipes to get desired results. Remember that every recipe is different, and any or all of these adjustments may be required. The suggestions here are only meant to be a rough guide—each recipe is different and you will need to experiment to see what actually works best for you. It will help if you keep notes of how you adjust recipes until you know what works best.

Because higher altitudes have lower air pressure, leavening agents (yeast, baking powder and baking soda) cause the gases in breads or cakes to expand faster, so baked goods rise faster (often over-rising then collapsing). One teaspoon of baking powder at 5,000 feet produces 20 percent more volume than at sea level. Bread also rises faster and must be watched.

The three basic adjustments for high-altitude baking are as follows:

1. Reduce Baking Powder
For each teaspoon decrease
> ⅛ teaspoon at 3,000–5,000 feet
> ⅛–¼ teaspoon at 5,000–6,000 feet
> ¼ teaspoon for 7,000 feet or higher

2. Reduce Sugar
For each cup decrease
> 0–1 tablespoon at 3,000–5,000 feet
> 0–2 tablespoons at 5,000–6,000 feet
> 1–3 tablespoons for 7,000 feet or higher

3. Increase Liquid
For each cup add
> 1–2 tablespoons at 3,000–5,000 feet
> 2–4 tablespoons at 5,000–6,000 feet
> 3–4 tablespoons for 7,000 feet or higher

Typically, all three of these adjustments are needed. Ingredients such as eggs or butter are considered liquids.

In addition to these changes, you should increase the baking temperature 15 to 25 degrees (unless using a glass pan) to help "set" the cell framework and prevent collapsing. You then may need to reduce the baking time by about 20 percent to prevent over baking.

Shortening can also be a problem. Too much fat in a batter will weaken the cell structure. The substitution of margarine for butter or shortening can noticeably affect the texture and produce an inferior taste. Solid shortening gives better results at this altitude because it holds more liquid.

Regarding eggs, higher egg content provides more protein for a better cell framework, so extra large eggs should be used. Without enough egg, the batter will be less stable and the final product will be too dry. Some cakes, especially angel food and sponge, require an even greater number of eggs. Also, eggs should be used at room temperature, and be careful not to over-beat them, as this adds too much air, aggravating the rapid-rising problem and the dryness.

Yeast bread

Most yeast bread recipes are reliable at most altitudes. However, since fermentation of sugar is faster at higher altitudes, breads rise much faster—in one-third the time noted for lower altitudes. Be careful that the dough does not rise more than double its bulk. Also, the faster rising time does not allow the flavor to fully develop. Punching down the dough twice instead of once will improve flavor as well as texture. Salt acts as a yeast retardant, so don't bake bread at high altitude without it. And don't use self-rising flour.

Another problem with breads at high altitudes is dryness. Decreasing the flour specified in the recipe just enough to make a stiff batter or soft dough that is handled easily (could be up to 1/4 less) will help make your bread less dry. Sifting flour can result in reduction of flour, and on a humid day could add some needed moisture. Whole wheat and "dark" flours require more liquid than white. Fresh fruits and vegetables add liquid to dough in the knead cycle. The more liquid (to a certain point) the more interesting, complex and varied the crumb and crust.

Bread machines represent another problem at altitude. To use the bake cycle in the machine, you must be very careful about the amount of additional liquid. Give up the "overnight" or time/delay mode. Gold Medal flour recommends using active dry yeast in lieu of bread-machine or Rapid Rise yeast. If the dough is coming out too dry, Fleischmann's recommends adding a couple teaspoons of water to the dough until it comes out in a tight, shiny ball. If the bread caves in on itself, reduce the yeast by 1/4 to 1/2 teaspoon.

Quick breads

Quick breads have various textures from muffin-like to cake-like. If muffins seem dry, reduce sugar by at least one teaspoon. Also, be careful not to over-mix, as this causes peaked tops rather than the preferred rounded tops. If you note a bitter taste, try decreasing the baking soda or baking powder slightly. Usually, both shortening and sugar can be reduced by as much as one-fourth of the total amount and still provide tasty bread. For biscuits, try adding a tablespoon of milk to each cup of flour and reducing baking powder slightly.

Cookies

Most cookie recipes yield acceptable results at high altitude, but many can be improved by slightly increasing baking temperature. Cookies with lots of chocolate, nuts or fruit may need a reduction of baking powder/soda by up to half. Also, cookie recipes often contain a higher proportion of sugar and fat than necessary. Up to one-fourth of the sugar can be replaced with nonfat dry milk without loss in quality.

Pie crusts

To get a tender and flaky crust, it helps to have all ingredients at 70 degrees (room temperature) and preheat oven. Handle dough lightly and no more than absolutely necessary. Too much flour produces a tough crust; too little makes it soggy. Sometimes, adding more liquid (up to 25 percent more but not so much as to make the crust soggy) helps to hydrate the flour. Using a non-shiny, metal pan generally helps achieve a good, brown crust.

Cake mixes

Follow the high-altitude adjustments given on the mix box. These have been tested to work with the mix's specific ingredients. You may still need to make a few minor adjustments; adding an egg is what you can try first.

Other High Altitude Adjustments

The boiling point
The important point to know about cooking anything at higher altitudes is that when the atmospheric pressure is less, the temperature required for water to boil is less. What boils at 212°F at sea level will boil at 208°F at 2,000 feet, at 203°F at 5,000 feet, 198°F at 7,500 feet and 194°F at 10,000 feet. Cooking food in water boiling at these lower temperatures takes longer, because the water is boiling at a lower temperature and thus the food is cooking at a lower temperature. For example, the "3-minute egg" will take more time. Also, a bowl of boiling soup is not as hot. The following are a few recommendations for specific types of cooking. Again, these are only meant as a guide; experiment and see what works best for you:

Candy making
To prevent excessive water evaporation while cooking, decrease your final cooking temperature by the difference in the boiling point of water for your altitude and that of sea level. This is an approximate decrease of 2°F for every increase of 1,000 feet in elevation. You may need to use a longer cooking time.

Deep-fat frying
The lower boiling point requires lowering the temperature of the fat to prevent food from over-cooking on the outside and under-cooking on the inside. The decrease varies with the recipe, but a rough guide is to lower the frying temperature about 3°F for every increase of 1,000 feet.

Puddings and cream pie fillings

Above 5,000 feet, the temperatures obtained with a double boiler are not high enough for maximum gelatinization of starch. Carefully use direct heat rather than a double boiler.

Miscellaneous other changes for altitude

In general, all stovetop and oven baked foods (if temperature not adjusted) take longer at altitude. Pasta needs a hard boil and will take longer; check for doneness by taste not time. Dried beans need to be cooked as much as twice as long as at sea level; a pressure cooker is a great help here. Slow stews need about one hour extra for every 1,000 feet above 4,000 feet. Baked items usually need higher cooking temperatures (which sometimes leads to shorter cooking times) and sometimes light covering with foil to help hold in moisture. Cooking bags are great for turkeys and roasts (follow directions that come with the bags and use a meat thermometer to insure doneness). Experiment and find out what works best for you.

INDEX

WHERE TO BUY CHILES

The chile products used in these recipes are widely available in supermarkets and specialty stores in major metropolitan areas around the country. If you have difficulty finding chiles in your locality, call one of these reliable sources. Many of them provide regular mail-order services. You can order from a number of them off the Internet, and some of these can even overnight you fresh or frozen green chile in season.

SOUTHWEST

Apple Canyon Gourmet
P.O. Box 16494
Albuquerque, NM 87191
505-332-2000
1-800-992-4659
www.applecanyon.com

Bueno Foods
2001 4th Street SW
Albuquerque, NM 87102
505-243-2722
1-800-95CHILE
www.buenofoods.com

Casados Farms
Box 852
San Juan Pueblo, NM 87566
505-852-2433

Chile Addict
325 Eubank NE
Albuquerque, NM 87123
505-237-9070
www.chileaddictstore.com

The Chile Shop
109 East Water Street
Santa Fe, NM 87501
505-983-6080
www.thechileshop.com

Chile Traditions
8204 Montgomery Blvd. NE
Albuquerque, NM 87109
505-888-3166
1-877-VERY-HOT
www.chiletraditions.com

Los Chileros
401 2nd. St. S.W.
Albuquerque, NM 87102
505-768-1100
1-888-328-2445
www.888eatchile.com

Da Gift Basket
P.O. Box 2085
Los Lunas, NM 87031
505-865-3645
1-877-468-2444
www.dagiftbasket.com

Graves Farm & Garden
6265 Graves Road
Roswell, NM 88203
575-622-1889
rgraves@dfn.com

Hatch Chile Express
P.O. Box 350
Hatch, NM 87937
575-267-3226
1-800-292-4454
www.hatch-chile.com

Hobson Gardens
3656 Hobson Road
Roswell, NM 88203
575-622-7289
Seasonal operation

Jane Butel's Pecos Valley Spice Co.
2655 Pan American NE, Suite F
Albuquerque, NM 87017
505-243-2622
www.pecosvalley.com

NM Chili.Com
2315 Hendola NE
Albuquerque, NM 87110
505-217-2105
1-888-336-4228
www.nmchili.com
wholesale:
www.wholesalechili.com

Pendery's
1221 Manufacturing Street
Dallas, Texas 75207
1-800-533-1870
www.penderys.com

Santa Fe Chile Co.
    See Apple Canyon Gourmet

Santa Fe School of Cooking
116 West San Francisco Street
Santa Fe, NM 87501
505-983-4511
1-800-982-4688
www.santafeschoolofcooking.com

WEST & NORTHWEST
La Palma
2884 Twenty-Fourth Street
San Francisco, CA 94110
415-647-1500
fax: 415-647-1710

EAST
The Hot Shoppe
311 S. Clinton St.
Syracuse NY 13202
1-888-468-3287 (HOTEATS)
www.hotshoppe.com

Mo Hotta–Mo Betta
P.O. Box 1026
Savannah, GA 31402
1-800-462-3220
www.mohotta.com

WHERE TO BUY NEW MEXICO WINES

Most of New Mexico's wineries are small to medium-sized operations. You can visit with the winemakers, who will be happy to let you sample their wines. Visiting these wineries or purchasing their wines at your local store gives you the flavor of New Mexico like nothing else. The New Mexico Vine and Wine Society (http://www.vineandwine.org/) and the New Mexico Wine Growers Association (http://www.nmwine.com/) are the two groups who promote the wines of New Mexico. A free detailed map showing the location of wineries in the Land of Enchantment is available free by writing to New Mexico Wine Growers Association, P.O. Box 3511, Santa Fe, New Mexico 87504. You can also find New Mexico wineries and maps showing their locations (as well as humorous descriptions of the wines) at http://wine.appellationamerica.com/wine-region/New-Mexico.html. Listed below is detailed information about New Mexico wineries, including web sites and contact information. For a good introduction to various types of wine, including serving suggestions, see www.wineintro.com.

One other piece of information to keep in mind is that it is still illegal to ship wine to some states; in fact, it as actually a felony in a few. To see if wine can be shipped to your state, see www.wineintro.com/basics/shipping. Shipping in and out of New Mexico is not a problem; you need to see if wine can be shipped INTO your state. Here is a list of New Mexico wineries that offer fine wines.

Anasazi Fields, Inc.
PO BOX 712
Placitas, NM 87043
505-867-3062
www.anasazifieldswinery.com

Anderson Valley Vineyards
4920 Rio Grande Blvd. NW
Albuquerque, NM 87107
505-344-7266

Arena Blanca Winery
7320 U.S. Hwy 54/70 North
Alamogordo, NM 88301
575-437-0602
www.pistachiotreeranch.com

Bees Brothers Winery)
619 Nowicki Lane
Albuquerque, NM 87105
Phone: 505-452-3191 message
www.beesbrothers.com

Black Mesa Winery
1502 State Highway 68 Box 308
Velarde, NM 87582
505-852-2820
Phone & Fax: 1-800-852-6372
www.blackmesawinery.com

Casa Rondeña Winery
733 Chavez Road NW
Los Ranchos de Albuquerque
NM 87107
505-344-5911
505-343-1823
800-706-1699
www.casarondena.com

Corrales Winery
6275 Corrales Road
Corrales, NM 87048
505-898-5165
www.corraleswinery.com

Gruet Winery
8400 Pan American Frwy NE
Albuquerque, NM 87113
505-821-0055
www.gruetwinery.com

Heart of the Desert Vineyard
& Tasting Room
Eagle Ranch 7288 Hwy 54/70
Alamogordo, NM 88310
575-434-0035
www.heartofthedesert.com

La Chiripada Winery
Hwy. 75 PO Box 191
Dixon, NM 87527
505-751-1311
www.lachiripada.com

La Viña Winery
4201 S. Highway 28
La Union, NM 88021
575-882-7632
www.lavinawinery.com

Las Nutrias Winery
P.O. Box 1156
4627 Corrales Road
Corrales, NM 88048
505-897-7863

Los Luceros Winery
P.O. Box 1100
Alcalde, NM 87511
505-852-1085
505-753-7925

Luna Rossa Winery
3710 W. Pine Street
Deming, NM 88030
575-544-1160
www.lunarossawinery.com

Madison Vineyards & Winery
HRC 72 Box 490
Ribera, NM 87560
575-421-8028
www.madison-winery.com

Milagro Vineyards
985 West Ella P.O. Box 1205
Corrales, NM 87048
Phone & Fax: 505-898-3998
www.milagrovineyardsandwinery.com

Ponderosa Valley Vineyards
& Winery
3171 Highway 290
Ponderosa, NM 87044
575-834-7487
www.ponderosawinery.com

Sandia Shadows Vineyard
& Winery
P.O. Box 92675
Albuquerque, NM 87199-2675
505-856-1006

Tasting Room:
11704 Coronado, NE
Albuquerque, NM 87122
(505) 298-8826

Santa Fe Vineyards
Route 1, Box 216A
Española, NM 87532
505-753-8100
800-477-2571
www.santafevineyards.com

Santa Rita Cellars
Wines of the Southwest
2641 Calle de Guadalupe
Mesilla, NM 88047
575-524-2408
877-NMWINES
www.santaritacellars.com

Sisneros-Torres Vineyards
P.O. Box 193
23 Winery Road North
Sabinal, NM 87006
505-861-3802
bert9436@msn.com

Southwest Wines
New Mexico Wineries Inc.
P.O. Box 1180
Deming, NM 88031
575-546-9324
www.southwestwines.com

Tularosa Vineyards
#23 Coyote Canyon Road
Tularosa, NM 88352
Phone: 575-585-2260
www.tularosavineyards.com

Vivác Winery
2075 State Highway 68
Dixon, NM 87527
505-579-4441
www.vivacwinery.com

Vina Madre Winery
PO Box 2002
Roswell, NM 88202
(575) 622-7070

Willmon Vineyards
2801 Sudderth Drive
Ruidoso, NM 88345
Phone: 575-630-WINE

Wines of the San Juan
Tasting Room
233 Hwy 511
Blanco, NM 87412
505-632-0879
www.winesofthesanjuan.com

ABOUT THE AUTHOR

Clyde W. Casey, who lives in Roswell, New Mexico, was born and raised in Colorado Springs, Colorado, of pioneer and Cherokee Indian heritage. Following attendance at Colorado College, he became a well-known author, professional entertainer, award-winning sculptor and energetic cook.

Art has been Casey's lifetime love and cooking—which he considers an art form—his special passion. His greatest sense of satisfaction and enjoyment comes from sharing his knowledge of New Mexico's colorful heritage and foods with others. He is the author of the award winning cookbook *Red or Greeen: New Mexico Cuisine.*

Involved in the art business for nearly 40 years, Casey was a sculptor of Western bronzes, an art gallery operator and a general promoter of the arts. A noted Western art historian and sculptural art restoration expert, he served for a number of years as president of the Professional Artists of Colorado. He also indulged his side interest—entertaining—by producing show segments for the Jaycee Chuckwagon in the Garden of the Gods Visitor and Nature Center by Pikes Peak. At one time he also picked guitar, sang, and wrote songs with a three-man group, the Trailriders.

Casey was involved in other ventures as well. He owned the first full-line pet store and grooming parlor in Colorado Springs. He also trapped rattlesnakes and shipped them live to a biological supply house for the production of anti-venom serum.

Always seeking new interests to challenge his inquisitive mind and intrigued by many visits to New Mexico, Casey made Roswell, New Mexico, his home about twenty years ago, helping to establish a bus manufacturing plant. He immediately began studying his new home state's history and culture. He retired in 2003 and now spends his time writing cookbooks and novels.

Clyde Casey lives with his wife, Millie, a prize-winning quilter, in Roswell. They have three grown children, five grandchildren and one great-grandchild. At home he works on perfecting his ever-growing collection of New Mexican recipes.

WINNER BEST COOKBOOK
NEW MEXICO BOOK AWARDS

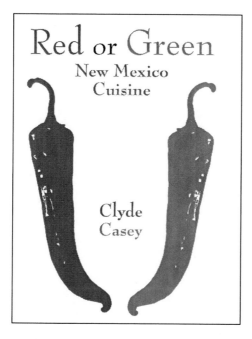

Red or Green
New Mexico
Cuisine

Clyde
Casey

"Red or green?" This is the most commonly asked question in New Mexico's restaurants.

In Red or Green: New Mexico Cuisine, author Clyde Casey helps you decide that question, offering more than 200 recipes for traditional and modern dishes from New Mexico. And while this book specializes in chile cuisine, it features wonderful recipes of all kinds.

You'll find the exotic—Blue Cornmeal Pancakes with Green Chile Chutney, Blackened Tomato-Mint Salsa—along with classics such as Beef Enchiladas and Green Chile Stew.

Game and fish recipes include Cherokee Venison Meatloaf as well as Crayfish Quiche and Pecan Coated Catfish. Desserts vary from the more familiar Rum Apple Crisp and Piñon Nut Cookies to the unusual—and unusually delicious—Chocolate Tortilla Dessert.

LaVergne, TN USA
08 November 2009
163379LV00004B/7/P

9 781574 160963